BUILDING BARCELONA

A Second Renaixença

by Peter G. Rowe

Peter G. Rowe is the Raymond Garbe Professor of Architecture and Urban Design and a University Distinguished Service Professor at Harvard University. After joining the Harvard faculty in 1985 from Rice University, Rowe served as Dean of the Graduate School of Design between 1992 and 2004. The author of numerous books, Rowe's work concentrates on cultural and urban-architectural aspects of modernization, principally in the Untied States, Europe and, of late, in East Asia.

8	EARLIER MOMENTS	9	Breaking Out of the Walls
		21	International Attention and Architectural Identity
		30	Years of Hunger to Years of Development

38	HOLDING THE LINE
44	TRANSITIONS

48	COLLECTIVE POSSESSION	48	Taking Back the City
		55	Urban Public Space Projects
		66	Affinity With Urban Architecture

70	PASSAGES
75	PLAZAS A PLENTY

82	OLYMPIC OPPORTUNITY	82	Lines of Command
		88	Olympic and Other Urban Projects
		103	Post-Games Hangover

110	JUST RAMBLING ALONG
114	DOWN BY THE SEA

120	BOLD TRANSFORMATIONS	120	Pushing Forward Again
		129	River to River Transformations
		142	Too Far, Too Fast?

148	GONE TO MARKET
153	MEANWHILE, DOWN AT THE FORUM

158	EXPANDING VISION	159	Towards Regional Metropolitanism
		168	Preserving Competitive Advantages
		176	End of an Era

188	HIGH ABOVE THE CITY
195	FROM HERE TO THERE

200	References

204	NECESSARY ABSTRACTIONS

208	Illustration Credits

Introduction

It is often said that Barcelona has been one of the world's most active cities over the last quarter century from the standpoint of urban planning. From the city's first small concrete squares in the 1980s to today's large-scale infrastructure to meet the challenges of the new global economy, Barcelona's development reflects a rapidly-changing world. It is small wonder then that our projects have covered every conceivable scale.

Some of our projects are well-known, like those for the 1992 Olympic Games. Others are not. However, rather than just focus on the showcase items, we also want to capture the overall transformation that has occurred in Barcelona. It is precisely because change is inevitable that we need to reflect on what has been done before planning ahead.

While Barcelona is often considered a shining example of urban planning, it is also true that a great deal still needs to be done (particularly with regard to tapping the opportunities offered by the new economy and globalisation). All Western cities exhibit more or less the same problems – something that becomes patently clear at gatherings of city mayors. While we all seek the same solutions, citizens want their city to reflect a unique collective identity. This dialectic makes managing urban change a tricky, politically risky business. Hence the need for critical voices stimulating the city's development and shedding light on Barcelona's triumphs and failures in the urban planning field. Accordingly, the city's policymakers foster active public participation in planning processes. While such participation is a great asset, we should also heed foreign views on Barcelona – not least because cities now play a vital role in spearheading relations between countries.

Barcelona has no wish to relinquish its position as a leading Mediterranean city but neither does it want to lose the features that make the city unique. Barcelona's response to globalisation and the New Economy should express this uniqueness, in much the same way as the city's variant of the Gothic style does.

Prof. Rowe knows Barcelona very well, has visited the city on many occasions, and has sat on juries and attended meetings with local faculty and architects. Furthermore, his academic work has made him an expert on the diverse urban problems of cities ranging from America to China. His work on Barcelona, under the title *Building Barcelona: A Second Renaixença* is therefore of capital importance. Prof. Rowe's insights into Catalonia and the European context are all the more acute because he has taken part in planning debates with key figures in Barcelona. Moreover, he has clear ideas of the role that the city could play on today's international stage.

Joan Clos
Mayor of Barcelona

Acknowledgements

This book came about because I was asked to write it, first by Josep Acebillo and then by Mayor Joan Clos. Frankly, at the outset I was very reluctant to acquiesce to their request, as I thought such an undertaking should be pursued by someone much closer and more deeply involved in Barcelona's city building process. Nevertheless, they prevailed on me principally by making the argument that they welcomed an outside perspective on the city – for that is surely what this book is about – by someone who had been around sufficiently and over a long enough period of time to make observations and advance arguments about what seems to have happened there. In fact, I first visited Barcelona, during my graduate student days in 1971, followed by a visit after the end of the Franco regime in 1978, before entering into a period of more frequent, yet intermittent engagement, beginning around 1987, when the Graduate School of Design at Harvard University, within which I was a faculty member, conferred its then Prince of Wales Prize in Urban Design on the city. This contact was then followed by sojourns during several summers on a variety of teaching assignments and, most recently, by participation in quality control commissions and other consultative roles on matters of design and urbanization for the City. I should also point out, if it is not obvious from this text, that Barcelona has exercised a continuing positive hold on my attention and affection almost from the outset, the latter response no doubt coloring my interpretation from time to time. For me, it is an extraordinary place.

Especially from the late 1980s onwards, I have had the good fortune of coming into contact with many dedicated practicing professionals, academics and members of government. Indeed, they are far too numerous to mention here all by name. Nevertheless, to Manuel de Solà-Morales, I owe a special debt for his continuing insight and for encouraging me, from time to time, to think of matters of urban design beyond my immediate context. In a similar vein, Rafael Moneo, my esteemed colleague at Harvard, after he left his teaching post in Barcelona, first got me seriously interested in the city, and over our years together has been a source of wise counsel and sense of high standard. From Eduard Bru, Josep Lluís Mateo, the late Enric Miralles and Elías Torres, I have learned much and gained a deeper appreciation of urban-architectural design. Also, Oriol Bohigas and Beth Galí have been very generous with their time and their cultured and nuanced views about the city. To Joan Trullén, I also owe a special debt for 'walking me through,' as it were, many of the economic and other statistical factors shaping Barcelona, especially of late. Eduardo Mendoza also offered valuable insights, beyond matters of design and planning, for which I am grateful. Then, there are three major protagonists in this story, as well as the story behind the story – Josep Acebillo, Joan Clos and Pasqual Maragall. Ace was not only an instigator of this enterprise, but a constant, almost encyclopedic source of information and font of effusive enthusiasm throughout. Moreover, his personal role in constantly trying to productively push Barcelona's urban enterprise forward must be admired. Similarly, both Mayors Clos and Maragall were welcoming, more than generous with their time and admirably frank in their opinions, for which I will always be grateful. Closer to home, on the research and production side, I would like to thank Carlos Anaiz and Clara de Solà-Morales – my two research assistants at Harvard – Maria Buhigas at Barcelona Regional for her help, and likewise my assistant in most matters, Maria Moran. Finally, to Joan Busquets, my close friend through much of this narrative and now Harvard colleague, I owe a great deal, both by way of guidance and particular insight, especially in reading draft material, as well as by way of unflagging support, especially when I was less sure about the efficacy of my efforts. Also, to Rosalia Vila and her partner Dorote Boisot, I am more than grateful for their uncommonly apt and interesting photographs, many of which grace this publication.

EARLIER MOMENTS

The fate of modern Barcelona has been and continues to be defined by a particular grasp on external events, a sense of Catalan nationalism, and by the ebbs and flows of an industrious and pragmatic-minded populace. As a provincial capital, the city has been engaged, sometimes disastrously, in the debate between the two Spains: progressive vs. backward, modern vs. traditional, secular vs. catholic, and liberal vs. authoritarian.[1] It has also sought, on several occasions, to escape the geography of this debate by reaching beyond Spain and appearing to be more international. Along the way, during the second half of the nineteenth century and early twentieth century, Catalanism, rooted in a reaction to eighteenth-century French hegemony and the later Peninsular War, became defined by a capitalist middle class on one side, and, secondarily, by socialism and to a lesser extent, anarchism, on another. More recently, since the Civil War and the demise of Francoism, this sentiment has been content to operate within Spain, especially among the socialists, although at times not without a strong hankering towards a kind of federalist autonomy. Leaders among Spaniards in industrialization and other facets of modernization, those in Barcelona pride themselves on being independent, hard working, commonsensical, although somewhat sentimental, and possessive of an instinct for propitious business outcomes. In short, they have – according to local parlance – *seny*.

Outward cultural manifestations of this admixture of social and political ingredients have been episodic and sometimes spasmodic. A combination of bourgeoise affluence, Catalan pride and gamesmanship gave rise to the outpourings of rebirth – *renaixença* – beginning around the 1830s, the general impetus of which gained in force and was transformed and continued through the later *Modernisme* and *Noucentisme* movements, well into the early twentieth century, although not without broader reactions, disputations and international orientations. Then followed periods of occlusion and dominance by larger Spanish interests, followed by an occasional outburst of local initiative and imagination, until the contemporary period, around the 1980s, which offered a 'second wind,' so to speak – a second *renaixença* – although again not without moments of collective exhaustion and casting about for fresh and revitalizing ideas. At stake, through most of this history, was the city fabric itself, the palpable and symbolic framework that orchestrates most Barcelonian's lives. For, unlike many other cities, Barcelona seems to have chosen architecture and urbanism as its most conspicuous, long-lasting and crowning glory.

Within this historical framework, the following narrative is largely about the past twenty-five years of physical development in Barcelona as a city and, now, as a broader metropolitan region. Essentially it chronicles urban and architectural events, as well as some of the motivations that lay behind them – the building of Barcelona in a continuing period of democratic governance, during which the city has effectively shaken off the often debilitating yoke of Franco's dictatorship. Progress in this direction, however, did not occur all at once, nor with complete force and again not without interruption. Nevertheless, from an overall perspective, re-possession and re-making of the city first proceeded gradually, then more confidently and, of late, almost over confidently, at least for some. Moreover, during specific moments of urban-architectural profusion, developments shared certain important similarities with those of prior episodes of resurgence, particularly those during the last half of the nineteenth through to the early twentieth centuries, despite the passage of time and notably different socio-political circumstances. Among these were: the creation of particular pretexts to experiment with grand collective projects and visions of the city, aimed, at least in large part, at international audiences; an unusual alignment and intertwining of local political will and architectural talent – often young – capable of producing and promoting innovative symbols of national or regional progress; periods of intellectual rehearsal followed by civic action, during intervals between repression and self-determination; and a marked capacity, among the city's leadership, for inculcating a sense of collective urgency, opportunity, and even crisis, to take on new projects, under both the guise and reality that Barcelona might be falling behind or not receiving its due, especially from Madrid and only slightly less so from elsewhere in Spain and in nearby Europe. Self consciously and not, a unique cultural *modus operandi* became established during the earlier days of modernization in Barcelona and, when sufficient freedom of operation was allowed, it later became a powerful means for pushing city building forward, especially during the latter part of the twentieth century.

Breaking Out of the Walls

In 1840 a liberal *Ajuntament*, the municipal government of Barcelona, debated the demolition of the *muralles* – the surrounding walls that, together with the *Ciutadella* or citadel of Barcelona, were a hated symbol of Bourbon tyranny over the city during the eighteenth century, as well as a severe constraint on its needed outward expansion. By this time many parts of Barcelona had become fetid, overcrowded industrial slums, as factories, co-mingled with residential structures rising four stories and more above poorly lit and inadequately-drained narrow streets and alleyways. High on the liberals' agenda was delivery of the city from appalling public health conditions, that included outbreaks of cholera, typhoid and dysentery and to relieve oppressive conditions for the working poor. They were joined by conservative businessmen with a desire to rid the city of its walls and citadel in the name of Catalan patriotism, if not by a sense of social justice, and because of the opportunities that would be presented for further real-estate development.[2] More specifically, the Ciutadella was a by-product of Catalonia's support for the losing side in the War of Spanish Succession (1701-1714), that pitted forces from England, Holland, Austria and Savoy against the Union of France and Spain under Philip V, the first ruler of the Bourbon dynasty. Designed and constructed by the Dutch engineer Prosper Verboom, between 1715 and 1720, the Ciutadella was a huge fortress on the east side of town, expressly aimed at keeping the populace in check, covering an area of some 60 hectares in a pentagonal shape, with artillery batteries at each of the five angles. At much the same time, in 1717, the enclosing walls of Barcelona went up and to make matters worse from a local perspective, construction of the Ciutadella resulted in destruction of La Ribera – a lively maritime quarter. Verboom also conceived of the Barceloneta, adjacent to the Ciutadella, which was intended as a barracks for troops, people expatriated from La Ribera, fishermen and port activities, although his designs were finished by Juan Martín Cermeño and construction began in 1753. In fact, at the time of the Ajuntament's initial debate about the walls, military installations in Barcelona covered approximately 50 percent as much land as civilian building.[3] Without immediate action, circumstances inside the walls continued to deteriorate pushing the Ajuntament, in 1846, to ban construction of any new factories. Finally, on August 12th, 1854 a Royal Order was issued authorizing demolition of the *muralles*. By 1855 this process was well under way, along with the Ciutadella a little later, and by 1865 only a few remains were left. In fact, rocks from the walls were used for paving streets and roads.[4] With practically everyone on their side, in 1859 a somewhat less liberal Ajuntament then held a competition for a new city plan beyond the walls, or what was left of them.

Although others, such as Josep Fontserè, were also involved, the two principal contenders for the new city planning commission, as events turned out, were Antoni Rovira i Trias and Ildefons Cerdà. Rovira probably enjoyed something of an inside track, as the municipality's architect and author of a prior study in 1864.[5] For the competition he proposed a scheme that appeared to defer to aspects of the old city, with five wedges of urban development fanning out from an axis extending inland from the Ramblas and generally creating a hierarchical organization of civic spaces. The Ramblas, incidentally, was by then a tree-lined avenue, running approximately through the center of Barcelona from the countryside to the sea, and a popular promenade for city dwellers. It was refurbished in 1776, again by Cermeño, out of a rough track and intermittent water course running between the two sets of walls enclosing the city.[6] In its well-mannered presentation of a tracery of public spaces, that clearly allowed for romantic interpretation, and its deference to the old city, Rovira's proposal was very much in line with prevailing conservative Catalan taste at the time, with something of a fixation on the 'glorious' period of the middle ages, when Catalonia was a dominant power.

Cerdà, by contrast, was not officially competing in the competition but developed a scheme in parallel, that hung in another room during the final presentation of proposals. He was a Catalan socialist who studied engineering in Madrid, between 1835 and 1841, moving back to Barcelona in 1849 to scrutinize the city, from which arose publication of *A Statistical Monograph on the Working Class of Barcelona* in 1856 and, later, his *General Theory of Urbanization and the Application of Its Principles and Doctrines to the Reform and Expansion of Barcelona*, in 1867.[7] He was also a friend of Narcís Monturiol, a fellow socialist and, among other things, an inventor of the submarine and an influential force in Barcelona's attempts at industrial and social modernization. Both imbibed the ideas of Étienne Cabet and Saint-Simon, the French philosophers and political thinkers. More pointedly Cabet, for whom Monturiol was a principal follower, in his *A Voyage to Icaria* of 1839 – a name later given to Sant Martí de Provençals, an industrializing area outside of Barcelona later named Poblenou – or simply 'New Town' – showed himself to be something of a pre-cursor to Marxism by asserting that 'law,' as a product of philosophy, could not be changed by mere voting and everything must remain in the control of the state.[8] Not far behind his friend in his enthusiasm for French ideas about an ideal scientifically-founded socialist community, Cerdà's proposal for extending Barcelona was a largely undifferentiated array of city blocks, or as one noted author put it "a Cabetian city of equal cells."[9] Covering nine square kilometers in area with 550 blocks around Barcelona, largely towards the hills and to the north-east, Cerdà's scheme made little to no reference to the old city. Instead, a rigorous rule structure was presented, based both on his prior and on-going empirical investigations of the existing city's drawbacks and upon other layouts of streets and blocks from elsewhere in the world. From these analyses a 113.3 square meter block was considered to be ideal, separated by 20 meter wide streets, for a nine square grid pattern – roughly a neighborhood – at 400 meters on a side, or easy walking distance. The corners of the square blocks were to be chamfered – the *xamfrans* – providing for better traffic circulation, more potentially active public space, as well as more light and air at street level. Further, a height limit of 18 meters was imposed, to be changed later in 1891 to 21 meters, and the allowable built area, within each block, was limited to 7,100 square meters of floor space, thus permitting passages and movement through the center of each block and ample open space for landscaping at the core of each block.[10] Likewise, the landscape along streets was envisaged to be both uniform and dense. Further, each district, within the scheme, was to be equipped with its own parks, hospital and schools. In short, Cerdà's proposal was almost the antithesis of Rovira's, both in its rational, as distinct from romantic, representational values and in the positivistic, as distinct from compositional, manner of its derivation. Indeed, it proved to be more generally influential and was referred to, for example, by C.M. Castro in his plan for Madrid of 1859 and 1869, along with other grid configurations.[11]

Perhaps not unexpectedly, given the relatively conservative temperament of those in power in Barcelona at the time, the Ajuntament selected Rovira's proposal in November of 1859. Afterall, it was also in their formal competition. Shortly thereafter in 1860, however, the central government in Madrid reversed the decision, awarding the commission to Cerdà instead. It's not at all clear why those in Madrid made this decision. It might have been because the more liberal authorities appreciated the equality of space proposed by Cerdà's alternative, as a more progressive manner by which to extend Barcelona. It might also have been because Cerdà had friends among engineers in Madrid – often powerful voices in matters of city planning – from his earlier sojourn there as a student.[12] Nevertheless, Isabella II layed the cornerstone of the *Eixample* (extension plan), as it then came to be known, in 1860, and further public works slowly got underway. These later included major traffic routes within the Eixample, like the Avinguda Diagonal, or simply 'the Diagonal,' parts of the Gran Via Corts Catalanes and the Avinguda Meridiana, as well as what amounted to a partial ring road in place of the wall, with markets, like Josep Fonsterè El Born market of 1873-76, and Elies Rogent's University of Barcelona of 1872, on its periphery. The tempo of private construction of the Eixample was also slow, not really gaining full momentum until the 1890s. Between 1860 and 1875 development was sparse, with concentration in a zone towards the right side, or *Dreta de l'Eixample*, immediately to the north-east of the old city, roughly bounded by the Rambla de Catalunya, the Còrsega, the Passeig de Gràcia, and the Gran Via Corts Catalanes. There was also some development in Sant Antoni, to the west of the Old City, and adjacent to the old wall, especially along the Ronda Sant Antoni.

Further development between 1876 and the 1890s was more dispersed throughout the Eixample, although often with relatively few buildings per block. In addition to further concentration in the inner zone, the area immediately in the direction of the left side, or *Esquerra de l'Eixample*, saw considerable construction. Also by the 1890s a concentrated corridor of development had emerged adjacent to the Rambla de Catalunya and particularly beside the Passeig de Gràcia, both leading out of the city up towards the hills. Contemporary records of *ad valorem* property taxation, for instance, indicated values that were almost double those of nearby streets and roads on both sides of this corridor, and records of the location of lawyers and other professionals also indicated concentrations along much the same corridor and within nearby zones of the Dreta de l'Eixample.[13] The 1890s, or thereabouts, also saw the arrival of a genuinely Barcelonian version of the apartment building constructed in the Eixample. Often rising seven stories in height, a ground floor with expansive floor-to-ceiling heights facilitated accommodation of commercial enterprises, with the *piano nobile* above supporting the opulent interior life-style of the well to do, followed, in section, by the remainder of the principal dwelling, apartments for rent and, finally at the top, by domestic quarters.[14] However, the Eixample of the 1890s and certainly of today, except in broad outline, is not what Cerdà originally envisaged. For instance, the ratio between built and open space within the blocks was obliterated by pressures for further real-estate development, often quadrupling the built area and filling in the landscaped cores of many blocks with additional structures, often housing commercial ventures.

Barcelona's belated breakthrough of its walls, for surely there was pent-up demand, was brought about by a mounting chain of economic, political and social events that went well back into at least the mid-eighteenth century, if not before, and principally, by the rise of the city as a center of manufacture. Earlier in the eighteenth century the loss of textile mills in Italy and the Netherlands profited the nascent textile industry in Catalonia, attracting cheap labor from the countryside into the city. By the end of the century, exports to the Spanish colonies had quadrupled in a short span of time and Barcelona earned the sobriquet of being the 'Manchester of the Mediterranean.' Around about the time of Cerdà's plan, Catalonia contributed fully 25 percent of Spain's

Gross National Product, becoming the fourth producer of cotton in the world, behind England, France and the United States. In fact, at that time, cotton textile manufacture represented 61 percent of Catalonia's industrial output, with engineering, often in the service of the textile industry, ranked second.[15] Industrial and other forms of entrepreneurial development were further spurred on by the establishment of joint stock companies – *societats anònimes* – in the late 1840s, that quickly experienced explosive growth during the 1850s and 60s. An Industrial Institute was also founded in 1848, headed by Joan Güell i Ferrer, both to promote and nurture Barcelona's secondary industry, and a Chamber of Commerce – *Junta de Comerç* – was established, although much later.[16] All was not plain sailing, however, as Catalonia and Barcelona experienced economic downturns during the depression of the 1790s and during the period of the Civil War in America in the early 1860s, when cotton feedstock for the mills was in short supply. Apart from recessional and related social impacts, those downturns also illustrated fragility in Barcelona's lack of industrial diversification, a characteristic that often continued to haunt the city up to the present day. The later economic fallout from the near extinction of the expanding wine industry, around 1890, caused by an aphid infection – Phylloxera – also illustrates this point. Curiously, for they were capitalist, traders and entrepreneurs of the first order, Barcelona's industrialists constantly sought protectionism for their cause. At first they lobbied Madrid with the claim that without protection they would surely be bought out by the British and then insisted on well-protected, almost exclusive rights for their enterprises. No doubt this attitude was also influenced by a sense of local traditional values, that set them apart, and by a suspicion of outside interference. Mostly, they got their way, primarily because it was also probably in Madrid's broader nationalist interest to have one strong example of industrial modernization, although free trade was enacted from time to time, such as during the First Republic, only to be rescinded again with the Bourbon Restoration in 1874.[17]

    The upshot of this industrial surge, was a reinvigoration of the Catalan spirit and the rise of Catalanism, after the region had lain virtually prostrate at the feet of its Castilian conqueror during much the eighteenth century. By the 1820s a marked tension existed between the moderately liberal, rising industrial values of Barcelona, which had been spared the Inquisition, and the conservative, often ultra-royalist sentiments of those in the countryside, who remained suspicious of almost all kinds of innovation. Indeed, this tension broke out in the first Carlist War, between 1833 and 1840, over claims by Carlos

María Isidoro de Borbón – the dead King Ferdinand's brother – to the Spanish throne and a return to absolute male monarchy over Isabella II. This grab for power was roundly supported by ultra-royalists and was to be repeated in two other Carlist Wars, between 1846 and 1849, as well as between 1872 and 1875. By 1840, with Barcelona well and truly on the make, two branches of Catalanism had emerged. The first and most dominant was conservative Catalanism, which was a form of pro-Catholic, yet anti-royalist, democratic capitalism, flowing from the ideas of prelates like the highly influential Jaume Balmes. The second was more radical, also involving cross-overs with socialism's international liberal idealism, that was leftist, anti-Madrid, because of the way the central authorities appeared to impede Catalonia's progress, and often intolerant of moderate liberals.[18] Proponents of this branch, varying in degree of radicalism and separatist fervor, were Pere-Felip Monlau and Pere Mata – two co-editors of influential socio-political tracts – as well as Abdó Terradas the socialist agitator who led the 1843 Jamància (Pastry cook's Revolt) attack on the Ciutadella in protest against city taxes. Certainly by the time of Cerdà's plan and through the last half of the nineteenth century and into the early twentieth, a division had emerged in Catalan politics between Catalanism, as a capitalist middle-class movement, and socialism and later, anarchism, seeking to follow broader liberal ideas and other forms of community action. During this period, with conservative Catalanism mostly in the ascendancy, Barcelona's entrepreneurs, rising middle class of professionals, small businessmen and larger shopkeepers, with the blessing of the *gent de bé* – those good families of the city – joined in sharing the rewards and lifestyle of Europe's bourgeoisie class. This also distanced Barcelona from the rest of Spain, which was largely cut off from European Enlightenment by Bourbon autocracy, and from nationalism arising from revolution and self-determination. Not that Catalonia was free of Spain, it was that its industriousness, nationalistic sense of identity and middle-class mores, were more like those in other parts of Europe.[19]

Apart from the political arena, Catalanism was also perhaps first and foremost a cultural enterprise, or at least it began that way in the 1830s. At that time, there was a resurgence of interest in legitimization of the Catalan language. Poets were needed and appeared in the likes of Joaquim Rubió i Ors and Bonaventura Carles Aribau, giving forth, respectively, with the *Bagpiper of Llobregat* and *La Pàtria*. Competitions among poets were organized – the *Jocs Florals* – beginning in 1859.[20] In effect, a movement emerged – the *Renaixença* – which soon encompassed not only Catalan as a language of culture but also of jurisprudence, university, publishing and journalism. At root, it was a conservative, medievalizing movement that celebrated ancient peasant traditions, folklore and evocation of popular history. Moreover, it was not a worker's movement but one that embraced the upper echelons of Catalonian society, enabling them to forge a nationalistic image for themselves against other parts of Spain and Europe. Its romanticism was also a means by which fears and anxieties coming forth from the onslaught of industrialization and modern change could be somehow arrested, or put aside.[21] By the last quarter of the nineteenth century, the movement died down, although the historicism and sense of regional identity that had been inculcated, at least among the middle and upper classes, was to continue through various forms of cultural eclecticism and habits of excursionism, by which those who were educated traveled to discover their own country – *Catalunya* – and to learn the values of it.

Another upshot of the industrial surge and the politics that went with it, was dramatic redistribution of population within Catalonia and particularly into Barcelona. When the city walls went up in 1717, Barcelona's population was around 37,000 inhabitants, living in relatively low-rise dwellings with only about 13 percent at four stories or above. By around 1800, inside the same walls, the population had risen to about 130,000 people, with over 70 percent of the dwellings four stories or higher. In the 1850s the city's population was around 190,000 with population densities approaching 900 people per hectare, or twice those of Paris, and with living space standards of about 9 square meters per person, comparable to averages to be found in China today.[22] Public health conditions, as mentioned earlier, were atrocious and the population was skewed strongly in favor of women, as many flocked to city mills from the countryside even as the lowest paid members of a burgeoning industrial labor force. Death rates exceeded birthrates, due to both high infant mortality and the lack of opportunities for marriage in a strongly Catholic society caused by the gender imbalance, and the city population was only buoyed up through immigration, mainly from other parts of Catalonia. Meanwhile, the Mendizábal Laws were enacted in 1837 – named after Juan Álvarez Mendizábal, who returned from exile to become a Minister of Finance intent on renovating Spain's stagnant economy – whereby some 80 percent of church property inside Barcelona was auctioned off – the *desamortització* – no doubt with some enthusiasm after the anti-clerical riots of 1835.[23] In addition, almost 30 percent of the arable land in Catalonia, then in the hands of the church, was bought by the rich bourgeoisie of Barcelona, resulting in a substantial recapitalization of agriculture, although still in the form of share cropping, largely because of the system's inherent efficiency for the new, largely-absentee property owners. This transfer of property was to have a significant impact. First, it placed more land in the hands of Barcelona's economic elite, now able to enjoy substantially more holdings both inside and especially outside the walls. Second, it placed into secular hands the vast majority of land in Catalonia and, third, it spurred on development inside, but more importantly, outside of the city. Combined with the ban on new factories inside the walls, less than ten years later the textile industry became substantially more footloose, settling in closer areas like Sant Martí, which had a population of 10,000 people in 1860 rising to around 35,000 by the 1880s, and in Sant Andreu, as well as in Llobregat.[24] While the walled city continued to be the major regional attractor, even though it meant living in appalling, overcrowded conditions for many, by 1860 and Cerdà's plan, the burghers, industrialists and other powers that be in Barcelona, could surely see the city's and their future lying beyond.

As mentioned, the rate of development of the Eixample moved slowly, with only marginal governmental commitment and a lack of financial resources in private hands – one of those pauses after a moment of urban reconceptualization and public works – although the tempo quickened as the century wore on. The churn of outside events, however, did not slacken. In 1868, a liberal coup, facilitated by the army under generals Joan Prim and Francisco Serrano, overthrew the Bourbon monarchy. Although Prim was assassinated in Madrid in 1870, the First Spanish Republic was proclaimed in 1873, with the Catalan Francesc Pi i Margall as its head. During this heady period of liberal reform, when Spain seemed to be catching up with the rest of Europe, a new constitution was formulated giving suffrage to males over the age of 21 years and generally disassembling many of the laws that separated the new from the old Spain. Republicanism did not last long, however, as the Bourbon monarchy was restored, bringing Alfonso XII to the throne in 1874, also catalyzed by the third and last Carlist War mentioned earlier, again with support from the Catalan countryside. Nevertheless, a socio-political watershed had been reached, especially in Catalonia, where the newly-rich speculators and stock traders, like Joan Güell, began to push aside the old nobility and traditionally-minded bourgeoisie. One source of the newcomer's power was wealth accumulated from the Spanish colonies in the New World, by the Catalan *indianos*, as they were called, and the *febre d'or* (gold fever) – stock trading – which ran roughly from 1877 to 1886, significantly expanding the Catalan economy.[25]

Later, returning to the growing tension in Catalan politics between conservative and radical factions, anarchists came to the fore, espousing a kind of authoritarian collectivism against the authority of both the state and the church, as well as calling for social responsibility through the dictates of public opinion. Indeed, during the early 1890s, Barcelona was seen by many to be the anarchist capital of the world, as the movement found a sympathetic response from peasants and industrial workers, poorly served by both the conservatives and liberals in or near power at the time. Acts of sabotage by the anarchists, however, led to their brutal suppression and the Montjuïc trials in 1896, that shocked the world. Meanwhile, far overseas, in 1895, Cuban separatists, led by José Martí, revolted against Spanish dominance. As events unfolded, President McKinley of the United States, issued an ultimatum for control of Cuba, in return for $300 million. Then, when the American battleship 'Maine' blew up in Havana harbor, the Spanish-American War ensued, including military actions by the American Admiral Dewey in the Philippines. When it was all over in 1898, Spain had suffered one of its most humiliating defeats, that also stripped the country of its colonial markets.

Political reaction in Catalonia, adversely effected economically by the Spanish defeat, was almost immediate. The already emergent power of the bourgeoisie, strongly influenced by the right-wing cleric Josep Torras i Bages, allied with regional ambitions of Enric Prat de la Riba, swept his party – the Lliga Regionalista de Catalunya – into power in Barcelona's elections of 1901 and then again in 1905.[26] Anti-Madrid in sentiment, the Lliga Regionalista was essentially conservative, sometimes hankering for application of traditional, rural Catalonian values to the industrial society of Barcelona, and deeply resentful of Spain's colonial losses. In 1906, Prat de la Riba published his *La Nacionalitat Catalana* – a regionalist, independently-minded tract – having written *Compendi de Doctrina Catalanista* in 1894. He then joined forces with members of the working class to form Solidaritat Catalana, winning a landslide victory, in 1907, taking fully 41 of the 45 seats available to Catalonia in the national legislature and nine of ten seats in the provincial government.[27] Some time later, in 1914, this 'regionalist' thrust continued further, with the creation of the *Mancomunitat*, the autonomous regional government of Catalonia – a Catalan state within Spain incorporating the provincial administration of Barcelona, Girona, Tarragona and Lleida, responsible for matters of health, culture, communications, transport, finance and education – something of a precursor of the present *Generalitat*.[28] As mentioned, however, by the late teens, the radical-conservative Catholic influence on Barcelona's politics began to wane appreciably. It was certainly struck a blow with the orgy of anticlericism, that erupted during the *Setmana Tràgica* (Tragic Week) of late July to August 1909.[29] Moreover, Torres i Bages died in 1916, along with the passing of a similarly-minded generation, including Joan Güell in 1918. In addition, the Setmana Tràgica was one of those left-wing eruptions that punctuated Barcelona's political profile. Sparked by the so-called 'Bankers War' in Morocco, requiring military support from Catalonia and, therefore, resisted by eligible workers, riots broke out and a general strike ensued against vested Catalan capitalist interests, also joined by left-wing migrant workers.[30]

During this period, from the turning of the nineteenth into the twentieth centuries, municipal authorities, entrepreneurs and civil society re-associated their interest in Barcelona, this time 'as a work of art,' much like prior and contemporaneous movements in other parts of Europe. The population of the city had almost doubled, since 1870, to 520,000 inhabitants, and the region, with just ten percent of Spain's population, was producing something on the order of 60 percent of its manufactured product.[31] In short, now there was political-economic wherewithal, matched by social ambitions and a sense of local, if not regional, identity. With the Lliga's rise to municipal power in 1901 an overall reform of the administration was undertaken, including its system of financing, and a much stronger involvement and commitment to planning and public services was pursued. In 1903, communication links from Barcelona to surrounding towns were established, with modern tramway service evolving from previous conveyances by 1910, extending as far as Sants, Sarrià, Horta, Sant Andreu and Sant Martí. Inter-regional railway routes, already linked Barcelona to some other parts of Spain by the 1860s, providing a substantial means for the import and export of the goods on which the city's industrial product depended. Further, in 1905 the city government sponsored a planning competition to more thoroughly resolve the connections between the Eixample and small nearby communities, such as Gràcia. In many quarters there was also dissatisfaction with the inherent monotony of Cerdà's plan. The competition was won by Léon Jaussely, whose plan, with its visual axes, urban perspectives, hierarchical arrangement of streets and representative public spaces, met the aspirations of the municipality for an ordered and monumental city.[32] It also met the organizational requirements of appropriately connecting the outlying smaller towns to the body of Barcelona and, overall, was substantially in keeping with the contemporary compositional principles of the City Beautiful Movement in the Unites States and the Stadt Baukunst of Centra Europe.[33]

Provision was also made to give spatial emphasis to major buildings and public institutions like the Hospital de Sant Pau and the Sagrada Família, both under construction, as well as the yet to be constructed concert hall – the Palau de la Música of 1905 to 1908 – and the north station – the Estació del Nord. In contrast to Cerdà, Jaussely thought of the city as a metropolis with multiple centers in a state of constant growth and change, and understood the necessity of an organized hierarchical distribution of urban activities, together with zoning, as a means for structuring social and economic life. His proposal, however was never put into effect, although it remained an influential blueprint in subsequent decades of local urban planning. The issue of connection to outlying areas was taken up again with the Merger Plan of 1917, although, here again, the proposal was not fully implemented. Meanwhile, per force of legal agreements, Gràcia, Sants, Sant Martí, Sant Andreu and Les Corts, had been effectively annexed to Barcelona by as early as 1897.[34]

Another proposal, however, that had lain fallow for a period of time was put into effect by the municipality and the Lliga majority in 1907. This was the 'Plan for the Inner Remodeling of Barcelona,' by Àngel Baixeras, that had gained at least tacit approval in 1889. A major contribution of the Baixeras proposal was the Via Laietana, running roughly along the edge of the old city – *Ciutat Vella* – on the eastern side through the Eixample, and providing an emphatic spatial link between the bulk of the city and the sea. Baixeras also appears to have moved beyond the insistent regularities of the Cerdà plan to an awareness of a metropolitan scale and an appreciation of Barcelona's topographic location on a rising plane between the Mediterranean and the Tibidabo – the foothills of the Serra de Collserola. By 1910, 'Garden City' ideas, popular in other parts of Europe and also in the United States, began to emerge in Barcelona, under the strong advocacy of Cebrià de Montoliu.[35] Indeed, the Parc Güell on a rise to the Tibidabo and one of the extraordinary works of Antoni Gaudí, was based, at least in part, on 'Garden City' principles.[36] Largely completed by 1914, the complex was to be composed of numerous private residential plots served by a common set of facilities, such as a market place, lighted streets, a public square and accommodations for a concièrge.

In sum, having finally broken out of the hated *muralles* in 1855, by the early twentieth century Barcelona had progressed and been guided mainly by the outlines of Cerdà's radical proposal for extensive territorialization. As other plans came and went, or were never fully realized, the city also gradually began to embroider the basic outlines of the Eixample, providing a greater degree of spatial differentiation and hierarchy among its parts, more scope for representative public spaces – both largely emulating *fin de siècle* inclinations in other major cities outside of Spain – and a broader sense of a metropolitan whole with specific topographic and social features. Outlying communities were more or less satisfactorily absorbed into the extending city fabric and municipal authorities in Barcelona, buoyed by a greater sense of autonomy and a higher level of civic commitment, firmly laid the foundation for a modern city. Progress in these directions, however, was far from even, as Barcelona was buffeted once again by outside events, internal socio-political tensions, and the sheer effort of carrying ambitious public plans forward against missed opportunities, an intermittent poverty of means, preoccupations with private enterprise, and adverse turns of fate.

International Attention and Architectural Identity

Intertwined with this city building process, often with the ambition of being regarded as a European 'capital,' Barcelona's entrepreneurs, architects, and civil authorities – more or less in that order – also pursued equally ambitious projects, that drew attention to their city and established a unique sense of architectural identity. The first pretext for such manifestations was the First Universal Exhibition of 1888, an undetrtaking initially promoted mainly by private enterprise, with strong participation by a group of international entrepreneurs specializing in prefabricated materials for mounting trade fairs and expositions. The site provided by the local government for the Exhibition was once occupied by the infamous Ciutadella, redevelopment of which began in earnest with a competition in 1869 and a final proposal for a park and garden by the winner, Josep Fontserè, in 1871. However, in 1887 a severe economic downturn forced the municipal government to take over organization of the Exhibition in order to save the city's reputation. Moreover, Rius i Taulet – the then Mayor of Barcelona who launched the Exhibition – also wanted to demonstrate that his city was capable of taking its place alongside others in modern Europe, well outside of the Spanish context.[37] Primarily, the economic downturn was due to the agricultural crisis that had a significant impact on the Catalan textile and wine industries mentioned earlier, as well as an ending to the *febre d'or*. Ambitious, though not overreaching, the main references for the Exhibition were not those that had taken place in major European capitals like Paris and London, but rather 'minor exhibitions' that took place in several European cities and had a direct impact on urban development, such as Brussels in 1882, Amsterdam and Nice in 1883, and Antwerp in 1885.[38]

Elies Rogent, the dean of the recently founded Escuela Provincial de Arquitectura in Barcelona, was engaged to pick up the pieces of the private enterprise, not to mention considerable debate, and to produce a master plan for the Exhibition and the Ciutadella site. In addition to the services of established architects, like August Font and Fontserè, Rogent also engaged younger talent in the likes of Lluís Domènech i Montaner and Josep Vilaseca, providing them with the opportunity to present innovative proposals. Rogent's plan consolidated the park and gardens of the Ciutadella site, providing a significant public access towards the waterfront and a large representational public space at the point of intersection between the old city and the abstract grid of the Eixample. His proposal also incorporated several older structures, such as: the Arsenal – remodeled by Pere Falqués – the remade parade ground, the Ciutadella Chapel and the Governor's Palace. Rogent also defined the urban conditions of adjacent approaches to the park and Exhibition site, especially the main entrance under a triumphal arch by Vilaseca. Various temporary pavilions, housing the bulk of the Exhibition, were set out in a semi-circular fan, at the southern end of the complex. Fontserè's Umbracle, a cast iron pavilion demonstrating use of up-to-date technology; the Park Café-Restaurant by Domènech i Montaner; and the cascade, lake and adjacent waterworks, again by Fontserè in collaboration with Gaudí, were among some of the more important local contributions. Indeed, Domènech i Montaner's restaurant was a striking eclectic piece of architecture at that time in Barcelona, appearing to react against the unifying influence of emerging modern cities and the universal abstractions of the current Art Nouveau, while simultaneously striking out towards a national, Catalan style with strong local roots.[39] The Exhibition also served as a pretext to introduce modern infrastructure to this section of the city, in the form of gas, electric light and sewage. Moderately successful, although perhaps not living fully up to all the city's expectations, the Exhibition lasted for 35 weeks.

Pursuit of a 'national,' Catalan architectural identity came to a head, around 1890, with the full advent of what came to be known as the *Modernisme* movement – a broad cultural reaction against the flagging movement of the Renaixença and the Jocs Florals and, in architecture, a break with prevalent Beaux-Arts practices of the Restauració. In literary circles the realism of, say, Zola was rejected in favor of the symbolism of a Mallarmé.[40] *Les Festes Modernites*, which helped give the movement its name, if not reputation, was first organized in Sitges – a seaside resort occupied in part by members of Barcelona's artistic community – by the painter Santiago Rusiñol, although an essence of the

movement had arrived earlier, when Domènech i Montaner published his essay, 'In Search of National Architecture' in the newspaper *La Renaixença*, in 1878.[41] Although not the same, exactly, as the Arts and Crafts movement, Art Nouveau, or Jugendstil, Modernisme was largely contemporaneous with these turn-of-the-century European outpourings, and, in architecture and in the decorative arts, looked to the past and especially to non-strictly Spanish Gothic and Arabic periods for inspiration. Basically, *modernista* ideology sought to give expression to the civilization of the day and embraced neo-medievalism, mystical symbolism and organic expressionism.[42] However, Modernisme did so in a manner that deliberately de-stabilized coherent architectural and artistic orthodoxies. It was the period that Pere Hereu defined as one of 'critical eclecticism,' whereby anything that was of value in the past was rescued and patched together in an amalgam of styles and building solutions, but ones that were selective and could be sufficiently manipulated and transformed to adequately express the spirit of the time.[43] In effect, the amalgam produced affects far removed from the historical stylistic starting points. Also at work, was a Wagnerian influence, rife at the time in Catalan culture, towards the experiential salvation of society from the toil and tedium of industrial life through the 'total work of art.' In addition, interests in technical research and new construction materials were evident, although, again, responses to emerging modern technology were furnished, following Gottfried Semper and, later, Viollet-le-Duc, by rethinking the future based on the past.[44] Common aspects of this cultural flowering in architecture were:
1) the importance attached to strictly decorative renditions;
2) adherence to known and stable building typologies, which were almost never subject to in-depth scrutiny or re-evaluation; and
3) a concern for the ornamental in an uninhibited, creatively intuitive and, often, sublime manner.[45]

Modernisme grew out of the Escuela Provincial de Arquitectura, which was founded in 1875, with Elies Rogent as a primary instigator, to supercede the Escuela de Maestros de Obras and to compete with the Escuela de Arquitectura in Madrid. Indeed, part of the pretext for forming the Escuela Provincial was a reaction against the hegemony of the Beaux-Arts regime dominant in the rest of Spain at the time. Between 1875 and 1885, Joan Martorell, Camil Oliveras and Antoni Gaudí – the so-called 'critical medievalists' – graduated from the Escuela. Other graduates also included Domènech i Montaner, Vilaseca, Antoni Gallissà and Francesc de Paula del Villar.[46] Actually, the terms *modernisme* and *modernista* were broadly introduced by J.F. Ràfols as late as 1949 to comprehensively describe the movement, only being used sparingly and often disparagingly at the earlier time.[47] Gaudí, for instance, always tried to distance himself from the label and stayed away from Sitges. Moreover, the spread of various architect's work, otherwise lumped under the *modernista* label, often reflected tensions in Barcelona among socially progressive secular and positivist inclinations, and among successional interests of the industrial bourgeoisie and conservative social Catholicism. Instead, the more neutral term *'fin de siècle* architecture,' proposed by Ignasi de Solà-Morales, probably better captures the architectural production, both by avoiding unnecessary distinctions and by more clearly referring the city's architecture to the broader movement going on in the rest of Europe, to which Barcelona aspired.[48]

There were three major proponents of this *fin de siècle* architecture. They were Domènech i Montaner, Gaudí, and Josep Puig i Cadafalch. A public figure throughout most of his professional life, Domènech i Montaner, the eldest of the three, was a promoter of the Catalanist directions of the Renaixença and the search for a 'national' architectural style. He was also a teacher at the Escuela in Barcelona and its dean between 1900 and 1920.[49] An architectural historian of note, Domènech i Montaner was something of a student of Gottfried Semper, as suggested earlier, and his four elements of building, namely:
1) the hearth as the center of social life;
2) the platform, from which building rises;
3) deployment of the roof and structural frame; and
4) walled enclosure, although not as a load-bearing structure.[50]
In these regards, he can also be seen as proto-modern by adhering to distinctions that did not otherwise apply among the sources of his eclecticism. His design, for instance, for the Montaner i Simon Editorial Office of 1881-1886, in the Eixample – now the Tàpies Foundation – is an ample demonstration of his proto-modern position, combining, as he did, an iron-framed structure, including a huge skylit roof, with elaborate patterned brick façades and large glass window openings with delicate wrought-iron tracery. Furthermore, Domènech i Montaner broke substantially with past attitudes towards urban design, by insisting on viewing the city as containing a diversity of urban functions, each requiring a particular architecture. Both the symbolic and functional layouts of his Hospital de Sant Pau of 1901, terminating a diagonal avenue deep in the Eixample, and the positioning and urban-architectural development of his Palau de la Música of 1905 to 1908, rather clearly illustrate this perspective.[51]

Moreover, the types of buildings and social programs in which he was involved – mainly public institutions, workshops like the Montaner i Simon office and the Thomas Building of 1895 to 1898, commercial offices like the Fuster Building of 1908, in addition to sumptuous private residences like the Casa Lleó Morera of 1905, again all in the Eixample – were, by and large, secular, modern in function, and bound up in Barcelona's progressive civic project of city making.

Gaudí, a contemporary of Domènech i Montaner, by contrast, was part of a cultural reaction to progressive, secular and positivist leanings in society. A devout Catholic, Gaudí saw redemption of the contemporary industrial city only by way of Christian content and the evocation of the virtues of an integrated medieval society. In these sentiments he was aligned within the conservative wing of Catalanism and very much a follower of Torras i Bages, who was invited as a spiritual advisor to the Cercle de Sant Lluc, founded in 1893 by Gaudí and the Llimona brothers. This group consisted of like-minded artists, architects and intellectuals with an emphatic concern for Christian values and a neo-medievalist attitude to social questions, somewhat like the English pre-Raphaelites.[52] In essence, theirs was a paternalistic social model of life, emanating from divine will and within which personal virtues of honesty, poverty and charity were to be valorized and pressed forward in a reformatory fashion. Apart from this association, Gaudí was something of a loner, although with strong ties to the business and religious establishment of Barcelona, at least for a time. In practice, unlike Domènech i Montaner, Gaudí concentrated most of his architectural efforts towards privileging the presence of religious and related social institutions – churches, schools, charitable foundations – through which the social message of Catholicism could be disseminated, as well as towards other projects of their patrons. Nevertheless, despite the confines of the architectural problems that he tackled and the ideological aims of his work, Gaudí left an indelible imprint on Barcelona and, indeed, ultimately on world architecture.

In his architecture, more than any of his contemporaries, Gaudí was consistently able to escape historicist references in order to pursue his own naturalistic and organic abstractions. In this pursuit he was enabled by an extraordinary and evolving understanding of building statics and material use, relying on intuitive insight, ingenuity and empirical testing, rather than on theoretical scientific knowledge.[53] Consistent with his ideological slant on life, Gaudí believed that such understanding was driven by revelation of the higher truths which the world of nature was capable of transmitting. In fact, through the repertoire of parabolic forms, catenary structures, vaults and buckled roofs on display in the Sagrada Família, the Colònia Güell crypt of 1898 to 1914, and the infrastructural support of Parc Güell, he appeared to be almost defiantly pushing past acceptable statical limits. Gaudí's work on the Sagrada Família began in 1884, when he substantially modified the original concept of a crypt, by de Paula del Villar, and remained incomplete when he was tragically killed by a tram in 1926.[54] Suspicious of new materials, Gaudí worked almost exclusively in stone, which he rendered in a variety of expressive manners, ranging from primordial, as in the grottoes and under-road arcades at Parc Güell, to a smooth, monotonic, almost cascading, wave-like format at Casa Milà, nicknamed *La Pedrera* – the quarry – and, among Gaudí's work, the building that perhaps most escapes historicist references.[55] Overall, Gaudí's formal expression and material installation was almost always organic and naturalistic, including decorative use of ceramic tiles – *trencadís* – again very evident in the balustrade seating surrounding the public plaza above the hyperstylar market place, on the gate house, and along the top of the walls at Parc Güell. Characteristic of other *fin de siècle* architects in Barcelona and as described earlier, Gaudí did not make substantial excursions into revision of available building typologies. In spite of the organic forms, the Sagrada Família, for instance, had a common basilican ground plan with five naves and a spacious apse. Again in spite of its expressive characteristics, a classical park repertoire of paths, roads, miradors, playing fields and a market place are to be found at Parc Güell. A possible exception to this conformity is the open-plan arrangement around two interior courtyards at Casa Milà, enabled by a rigorous structural system of pillars and metal joists connected to a self-supporting facade. By about 1911, Gaudí's ideologically like-minded patrons lost influence and also began to pass from the scene, and his commissions dwindled. He died in relative obscurity and poverty, having never married, and is now on the verge of being made a saint by the Vatican.

Puig i Cadafalch, the youngest of the three major proponents of *fin de siècle* architecture in Barcelona, by almost a generation, was raised in the Catalan national youth movement and, in addition to his architecture, went on to become a significant public figure. He was a city councilor in Barcelona between 1902 and 1905, a Catalan member of the Spanish parliament between 1907 and 1909, and a member of the Mancomunitat from its inception, serving as President in 1917.[56] A member of the mainstream of the Lliga Regionalista, Puig i Cadafalch's architecture was rather persistently neo-medievalist, apparent in the Codorniu Wine Cellars of 1901 to 1904, and in the Macaya House in the Eixample of 1901 – a Gothic-styled town mansion, with decorated stonework concentrated around its apertures and crowned by a crenellated roof parapet. Certainly more tempered in identifiable historicist direction than the work of Gaudí, the architecture of Puig i Cadafalch, at least in his earlier days, appeared to concentrate on figurative treatment, once the basic volumes and façade outlines had been established. This is very apparent in the ornate band of neo-gothic fenestration that stands proud of the main façade in the Palau Quadras of 1899 to 1906 and in the free treatment, with symmetries and asymmetries, of the façade of the Casa Amatller of 1898 to 1900, with its surprising stepped crown, decorated by ceramic tiles and a blending of gothic and vernacular traits. Nevertheless, like Domènech i Montaner, he displayed considerable skill in his urban understanding of the particularities of sites and in a rational conception of building plans and volumes. The Terrades Building of 1903 to 1905, well illustrates both points, with a rigorous plan fitted into an irregular site, where the Diagonal runs through the Eixample, surrounded by neo-Gothic archways along a continuous perimeter gallery and compositionally crowned by several large semi-circular tower elements. Puig i Cadafalch was also a transitional figure in architecture, obviously beginning to lose patience with the strictures of Modernisme, as the first decade of the twentieth century wore on. While neo-gothic resemblances are there to be seen in the serial arrangement of large window openings surrounded by skillfully-worked brickwork pilasters and pinnacles at his Casarromona Yarn Factory of 1909 to 1911, the overall affect is more abstract and rationalistic than much of his previous work. Certainly by the Development Plan for the Plaça Espanya of 1917, Puig i Cadafalch had turned the corner, so to speak, into the throws of *Noucentisme*.

In general, *fin de siècle* architecture in Barcelona gave form and expression to the city and especially to the Quadrat d'Or – development within the 'golden square' of the Eixample, immediately adjacent to the Ciutat Vella. Moreover, it did so in a manner that reflected Barcelona's new-found political autonomy, municipal wherewithal, private wealth, and sense of cosmopolitanism, as well as Catalan nationalism. In addition to architecture, it was a time when artisanal crafts flourished – including street furniture, mosaic work and marquetry – extending local traditions. These contributions were strongly evident, within the urban scene, for instance, in the prolific wrought-iron work of Josep M. Jujol, that also often graced many of Gaudí's buildings; the lamp standards by Pere Falqués along the Passeig de Gràcia of 1906; and in similar installations within the Plaça Real of 1899, by Gaudí himself. Common neo-medieval and naturalistic proclivities, that looked both 'backwards and forwards,' so to speak, were aimed to arrest the leveling influences of urban industrial modernity and to provide local specificity and identity. In this regard, architecture elsewhere in the world by, for example, William Butterfield in England, Anatole de Baudot in France, and H.H. Richardson in the United States, come to mind.[57] Throughout, functionalism took on a pre-modern meaning, representing engagement of the senses, the mind and the organic unity of the world, rather than revealing structural integrity, material capability and user utility.

Noucentisme which followed, was also a cultural movement effecting many areas of artistic activity in Catalonia, until the early 1920s. The term was coined by the philosopher Eugeni d'Ors and was used to qualify architecture that reverted to classicism, an interest in the civic qualities of urban life, and a certain amount of pre-rationalist, purist volumetric experimentation.[58] The *noucentistes* also had a 'nationalistic,' or regional, orientation, linked to a perceived Mediterranean tradition of a culture of humanism and related historicist values. Indeed, Renaissance codes of building composition were actively recuperated and all aspects were more or less well-defined in the School Units of the Mancomunitat of 1917, by Josep Goday, and in Nicolau M. Rubió i Tudurí's work at the New Benedictine Monastery of Verge de Montserrat of 1922, as well as in the Plaça de Francesc Macià landscape and building complex of 1923. Loosely associated with the regional government of the Mancomunitat, Noucentisme encouraged a culture of order, civitas and normality, befitting an era of relatively stable governance and steady social progress.[59] It was, in essence, a reaction to the individualistic romantic, spontaneous and process-oriented tendencies of *fin de siècle* architecture, in favor of classical biases and idealized aspects of urban form, that were not only to give shape but also to provide guidance to what many referred to as a new twentieth-century spirit. However, the movement was not entirely unified. Classicist aspects of the Vienna Secession, for instance, influenced Rafael Massó and Josep Maria Pericas, whereas a stricter classicism marked the work of Adolf Florensa – in the Cambó apartment building of 1921 – and of Francesc Folguera – in the Ritz Hotel of 1917 – as well as the work of Rubió i Tudurí.

The Universal Exhibition of 1929 was to be another showcase for Barcelona and an excuse for urban redevelopment of a peripheral area both on and in the vicinity of Montjuïc. The idea for another trade fair, originally set for 1914, was first proposed in 1907, with combined public and private investment, drawing on a lesson learned from the 1888 Universal Exhibition.[60] A plan for the trade fair and urban improvements was prepared in 1917 by Puig i Cadafalch, but disputes between the municipal and central governments led to postponements. Eventually, Rubió i Tudurí produced an overall plan for Barcelona, closely following Jaussely's earlier proposal, but departing from both Cerdà's and Jaussely's plans by considering the Plaça Espanya as the main center of the city, rather than the Plaça Glòries Catalanes – a commonsensical decision, at least at the time, given the Plaça Espanya's location on a major axis of the city and its proximity to nearby Sants Railroad Station.[61] The Parc Montjuïc was also constructed, as a part of the major park system contemplated by Rubió i Tudurí, from the top of which the overall 'grandeur' of Barcelona below was on view. Jean-Claude-Nicolas Forestier was engaged to plan part of Parc Montjuïc, leading up the slopes from Poble Sec, near the coast, through a series of terraces. By the time the Second Universal Exhibition was opened in 1929, the political scheme of Spain and the outlook for Barcelona had changed appreciably. In 1923, Miguel Primo de Rivera became the military dictator of Spain and the Mancomunitat was abolished shortly thereafter. This turn of events was not unduly repressive for Barcelona, however, and by 1931 Catalan was accepted once again as an official language, after Primo de Rivera's fall in 1930, ushering in the Second Republic along with the Autonomous Catalan Government – the *Generalitat* – first under Francesc Macià, from 1931 to 1933, and then under Lluís Companys, from 1933 to 1939.[62] Nevertheless, the overtones of the Universal Exhibition, that was opened by Alfonso XIII, were very much dictated by the central government in Madrid. Architecturally, it was also the occasion when Mies van der Rohe's radical German Pavilion ushered in the avant-garde to be taken up, in 1930, by GATCPAC (Catalan Artists and Technicians Group for the Progress on Contemporary Architecture) under Josep Lluís Sert, Francesc Fàbregas, Ricardo de Churruca and Josep Torres i Clavé, also known as GATEPAC. Strongly influenced by Le Corbusier, this group sought to give rational modernist form to what they perceived as being the potential for progressive and democratic culture under the Second Republic. They also collaborated with Le Corbusier on the Macià Plan for Barcelona, proposing maxi grids, as extensions to Cerdà's plan, and the zoning of major precincts within the city.[63] In tune with the avant-garde elsewhere, prototypes for workers housing were also proposed, such as the Casa Bloc by Sert, Torres and Joan Baptista Subirana of 1932 through 1936. On almost all fronts, however, an era had come to a close. Overall, the Mancomunitat had not been a very successful experiment and at one stage had to go into debt, due to a lack of sufficient financial support.[64]

Years of Hunger to Years of Development

Following a revolt against the Republican government, the Spanish Civil War broke out in 1936 and, three and a half million lives lost later, ended in Barcelona with the Republican defeat of 1939 and the ascendancy of Generalísimo Francisco Franco. To describe Franco's victorious regime as fascist is not far from the mark, although not entirely correct. Certainly the Falange – Spain's Fascist Party – was one of several factions within the regime, along with elements of the army, the church, and two other groups: those who wanted to restore the heirs of Alfonso XIII who left in 1931, and the Carlists. In practice, these factions were sometimes referred to as the 'families' of the Franco regime and included overlaps, such as either Catholic or Falangist generals.[65] More or less from the outset, what Franco managed to accomplish was a fusion of the various factions together into the *Falange Española Tradicionalista y de las Juntas de Ofensiva Nacional-Sindicalista*. This ensemble then became known simply as the *Movimiento Nacional* – the only lawful political entity in Spain, with Franco as the Caudillo, or unassailed dictator. However, over time, the Falange did become the dominant influence on Franco, primarily because of their more comprehensive political philosophy and capacity for governance, with an emphasis on national economic development, especially around agriculture rather than on industry. Although this proved to be ruinous, at the time Spain had little other choice. At the end of World War II, during which Spain was neutral, although, if anything, favoring the Axis powers, the victorious Allies had little incentive to provide aid and were in no mood to do so. Quite the contrary, when in 1946 the newly created United Nations passed a resolution to boycott trade with Spain, together with the damage and privations of the Civil War, real income per capita in Spain plummeted to nineteenth-century levels. Essential services dwindled, with, for instance, electrical supply in Barcelona only available for three to four hours per day. Food was also in short supply and, indeed, full scale famine was only averted by loans from the sympathetic Argentine dictator, General Perón.[66] Consequently, the late 1940s became known as the *años de hambre* – the years of hunger.

Meanwhile, Franco's animosity to Barcelona was particularly aggressive. For one thing, it had been the final redoubt of the Republicans and a principal source of resistance, throughout the 1940s and early 1950s. In 1944, for instance, the Communists made a disastrous attempt to invade Spain through the Valle de Arán. From 1947 to 1949, anarchists from Catalonia engaged in a campaign of shootings, bombings and hold ups which, although futile, also made Barcelona a target for the regime's ire. Then violence turned to mass protest, during the 1948 Enthronement of the Virgin of Montserrat, conducted in Catalan, and as a sign of protest against Franco by some 100,000 people.[67] The symbolism of the event was certainly not lost on the regime, which earlier had conducted a campaign against the Catalan language, barring its use in public institutions, destroying books, including historic collections, and insisting on Castilianized street signs and other place names.

In 1951, mass protest continued in Barcelona, with the first city-wide general strike in post-war Spain. Then, there were also members of Barcelona's Republican ruling class and assorted intellectuals, who went into exile following the defeat, but persisted with a shadow government. After Companys' execution in Barcelona in 1940, Josep Irla, who had been elected as the President of the Parliament in 1938, assumed the Presidency of the Generalitat in exile, a post he held until he resigned in 1954. He was followed by Josep Tarradellas, who was elected in a meeting in Mexico City's Spanish Embassy, a relatively safe place as the Republic of Mexico did not recognize Franco's regime.[68] Nevertheless, *seny* prevailed among many Catalans, after earlier outbreaks of its opposite – *rauxa* – violent reaction to the more prized traits of realism, earnestness and tolerance. In fact, many Barcelonians kept their heads down and went about their business, whereas others were not unduly unsympathetic to aspects of Franco's regime. The centrism and suspicion of Madrid was hardly new, although the diminution of support for industry, on which Barcelona depended, did not help matters. Moreover, as still a relatively rich region in Spain, Catalonia and especially Barcelona, attracted some 250,000 immigrants during the 1940s, straining still further the capacity for the city to cope in a time of extreme economic depression and demoralization.[69]

Although the United Nation's blockade and particularly American withdrawal from Spain ended in 1950, the Falangists continued to pursue insular and ineffective doctrines of development. Industry, for instance, was cloaked in walls of tariffs and quotas, virtually excluding the availability of needed foreign technology and related means of modernization. National income only regained Civil War levels in 1951 and it was not until 1956 that income returned to the level of 1936.[70] Immigration, now from as far afield as Andalusia, inundated Barcelona with about another 500,000 people during the 1950s, resulting in shanty towns – *barracas* – springing up on the city's periphery and on marginal lands, like the slopes of Montjuïc. Almost uniformly, these squatter settlements were built of make-shift materials and were without electricity, running water or sewage. Then, in 1957, with Franco's regime virtually bankrupt, Falangist ideologies were forced to give way to a new breed of technocrats, often from other 'families' within the regime. Indeed, many either belonged to or sympathized with Opus Dei – a sort of Catholic free masonry – seizing the opportunity to return the influence of the Church before circumstances again eluded their grasp. Largely from their hands, the 1959 Stabilization Plan was framed, which rather quickly proved effective in fighting run-away inflation and repairing the national balance of payments.[71] They also set in motion a gradual opening up of Spain to foreign investment, including needed modern technology and managerial practices. However, results were slow in coming and the measures of frugality needed to fight inflation and replenish the national coffers imposed further hardship on large segments of the population. This was so much so that many Spaniards migrated abroad and, indeed, were provided with incentives to do so, returning cash remissions which, in themselves, became a primary source of national income, along with tourism.

Another consequence for Barcelona of the end of autarky in 1950 and liberalization with regard to the outside world, coupled with immigration and hedges against inflation, was substantial growth in property speculation. In an effort to manage expansion, the 1953 County or Regional Plan and zoning stipulations of Josep Soteras and Pedro Bidagor were approved and put into effect.[72] Essentially, this plan extended the idea of the city to the outlying municipalities of Besòs and Llobregat, on either side of Barcelona, and incorporated a spatial logic of specific nodal pockets and complexes of urbanization aimed specifically at controlling the rate of urban growth and sustaining a viable urban model in concert with the existing city. A little earlier, in 1950, Grup R – a Catalan group of architects – became active in Barcelona. This group, which included José Antonio Coderch, Oriol Bohigas, Joaquin Gili, Josep Martorell, Antoni de Moragas Gallissà, and Josep Maria Sostres Maluquer, was first formed through a competition, organized by the local architects' association – the Colegio de Arquitectos de Cataluña y Baleares – in 1949 to solve some of the pressing housing problems in Barcelona.[73] For them the development of architecture and urban planning was based not only on technical, but also on socio-economic considerations. Ideologically they had a perspective that was inclusive, aimed at satisfying social needs – not surprising, given the times – with a lack of formal bias. Outstanding among their activities were the exhibitions held in the Galerias Layetanas in Barcelona, in 1952, 1954 and 1958. Influenced by Bruno Zevi and Alvar Aalto, among others, the group re-opened discussion of the modern movement in Barcelona, with interests in architecture of a strong local character to be found, at the time, in Italy and Finland. Associations, through Coderch and Federico Correa, with Team X were also influential and members of Grup R were instrumental in re-organizing the School of Architecture, with broader course offerings in urban development and in the social sciences. Architectural projects from members of the group were largely residential in character, including the Casa de la Marina Apartment Building of 1952 and the Tàpies House by Coderch; an apartment block for steelworkers of 1955 by Bohigas and Martorell; and the Park Hotel of 1950, with its cantilevered balconies, by de Moragas and Francesc de Riba. Also part of the cultural revival in Barcelona was Dau al Set, or 'die at seven' – an artistic and literary group, active from 1948 to 1956, including Antoni Tàpies and Joan Brossa, that based their stance largely on Dada and Surrealism, in opposition to the contemporaneous tastes within academic and official artistic circles.[74]

By the early 1960s, Spain's economy began to expand, ushering in the *años de desarrollo* – years of development – that spanned from 1961 to around 1973. Income per capita quadrupled and by 1963 or 1964 reached a level sufficient to remove Spain from the ranks of what the United Nations defined as being 'developing nations.'[75] In fact, the economy grew at an astonishing rate of about seven percent per annum, second only to Japan in the West, and by 1973 Spain had become the ninth ranked industrial power in the world. People were far better off in their material standards of living. Many families enjoyed a full range of modern conveniences, had better diets, and one in ten owned a car, compared to one in one hundred during the depths of the *años de hambre*. However, while expanding rapidly, the basic structure of the economy did not change appreciably. Only five provinces, including Barcelona, accounted for 45 percent of total economic output; the scale of enterprises remained low, with 80 percent smaller than five employees; productivity was roughly a half of the European average; unemployment was still relatively high; and investment in new industrial technology remained skimpy.[76] Although substantial economic gains had undoubtedly been made, per capita incomes for Spain, at the end of the *años de desarrollo*, were around half those of the average across other European countries and about one third the level to be found in the United States. In short, Spain remained a relatively poor country, when compared to other major Western counterparts and, while the lot of the urban middle class improved often due to invisible earnings, the two Spain's of rich and poor persisted. Finally, the *años de desarrollo* came to an end in 1973, spurred on by the OPEC oil crisis, which doubled the size of Spain's trade gap, and by a substantial downturn in tourism, as well as the return of around one million Spaniards working abroad, including their cash remissions. In 1974, the cost of living began to rise again, posting a whopping seventeen percent gain on the prior year.[77]

Throughout the *años de desarrollo*, the population of the City of Barcelona continued to expand, largely again through immigration from poorer Spanish regions. In fact, immigration peaked in 1963 and 1964, at around 45,000 newcomers, before tapering off through the remainder of the 1960s.[78] By 1970, the municipality had reached a population of 1.74 million inhabitants. Expansive though this population growth proved to be, it was actually the second largest wave of immigration in both relative and absolute terms. Between 1920 and 1930 the largest wave of immigration took place, largely from neighboring areas, like Aragon and Valencia, expanding the city's population by roughly a third. Then, the primary attraction was construction of Barcelona's subway and, of course, the Universal Exhibition and related public works. Certainly, by 1970, the number of native Catalans with deep roots were very much in the minority, both raising some tensions especially with less well-enfranchised newcomers, and diminishing the overall thrall of Catalanism as such. Nevertheless, the new would-be workforce entered into city life, as best they could. Many earlier immigrants traded up from their appalling shacks to newer low-cost, high-rise apartments, while others took their place. Some original squatter settlements also began to be upgraded and, by and large, land speculation and the indiscriminate building boom continued, departing appreciably from the orderly plans of prior eras. Stark, multi-storied apartment blocks began to appear on the outskirts of Barcelona, often without adequate amenities and infrastructure. Sponsored, at least in large part, by the financial mechanisms of the Plan Nacional de Vivienda, that aimed to produce four million new dwelling units in Spain between 1961 and 1971 mainly for sale rather than rent, these units were snapped up by all and sundry, often as a source of income.[79] One way to pay for the mortgage on the units was to take in lodgers. Indeed one estimate, provided by Francesc Candel in his bestseller about Barcelona's immigrants titled *Els Altres Catalans,* was that fully a fifth of all working class families were living in someone else's apartment. On par though, the real failure of the Plan Nacional de Vivienda was not the amount of dwelling units produced, for it exceeded its target, but the lack of control over property developers with regard to adequate provision for lower-income families. One estimate, when the Plan was over, placed fully 65 percent of the recipients among middle and upper-income families.

Another aspect of the *años de desarrollo* was the emergence of high-rise commercial building in Barcelona for the first time. Laissez-faire attitudes on the part of city officials combined with rising land rents, because of few superior locations in an otherwise constrained city, pushed a number of buildings well above the normal height of the surrounding urban fabric. Moreover, some, like the Torre Colón by Josep Anglada, Daniel Gelabert and Josep Ribas of 1965 to 1971, were free-standing skyscrapers, in the manner of modern American central cities. Rising more than 30 floors on a generous podium base, this rather conventional tower was capped with a different geometric form, further enhancing its apparent height. The Banco Atlántico Office Building by Francesc Mitjans and Santiago Balcells of 1966 to 1969, was slightly less tall, at some 25 stories in height, although dwarfing the neighboring buildings. With a plan and curtain-wall external structure, modeled after the Pirelli Building by Gio Ponti in Milan, some acknowledgement of local context was made by adaptation of the plan form to create a chamfered corner, typical of the Eixample. The building's location on the broad Diagonal also helped to diminish its scalar impact. The Torre Atalaya Apartment Building by Correa and Milà with José Luis Sanz Magallón of 1966 to 1973, although not exactly free standing, had a plan form that was omni-directional. Rising some 25 floors above grade, the reinforced-concrete structure and repetitive prefabricated elements gave the overall composition something of a Milanese and perhaps Brutalist appearance, not surprising given the times. In fact, many of the high-rise buildings in Barcelona were derivative, in one way or another, of prevalent international styles of commercial construction. One exception, perhaps, was the ensemble of four smaller squat towers – the Trade Office Towers of 1966 to 1969 – by Coderch and Manuel Valls. The curvilinear plan forms, sheathed in a sheer, glazed curtain walls, were arranged well within an otherwise difficult site geometry, partly inscribed by a major roadway. Nevertheless, the single-sized glazing module and the unusual form of the overall composition, at least in Barcelona, gave the complex a singular hermetic quality in appearance.

Amid much of this residential development and the building boom taking place in many quarters of the city, it became clear that urbanization was inadequately controlled and that regional and other urban plans were simply being overrun. In 1968, the Directive Plan for the Barcelona metropolitan area was proposed, although various analyses of the city's circumstances had begun earlier in 1964 and 1966.[80] Authored by the Barcelona Planning Committee, the Directive Plan was largely a re-think of the 1953 Regional or County Plan. However, the Directive Plan proved to be too general, lacking sufficient specifics for direct implementation, and was treated largely as a consultative document. A little later, in 1970, Barcelona Año 2000 was prepared by Xavier Subias, Francesc Escudero, and Antoni Riera at the behest of Mayor José María Porcioles. For some time Porcioles had been championing the idea of Barcelona as a 'capital city,' finally getting the central government to accept the proposition for yet another universal exhibition for 1982. This proposal was never developed, but its impetus was used as a means for defining the urban transformations published in *Barcelona Año 2000*. Characterizing Barcelona as the center of a metropolitan area of 6.5 million inhabitants, the proposal was largely aimed at giving further direction to what was already in play, addressing pressing issues like traffic congestion and expanding the territorial scope of ideas about road networks and public infrastructure. Barcelona's metropolitan population is still far from 6.5 million inhabitants, illustrating some of the hubris of Porcioles and his aggrandized ambition. Indeed, the rampant property speculation and building boom taking place in the city was enabled by the municipal government, subsequently earning the pejorative label as 'La Barcelona de Porcioles.'[81]

On the 20th of November 1975, Franco died, quickly followed by the din of whispered speculation about what might happen next, as for so long he had been the maker of all important political decisions that effected the country. This was a particularly anxious time for Barcelona, frowned upon for so long by those in power and, in turn, because of the city's long standing suspicions about what might issue forth from Madrid. However, it quickly became evident that Spaniards almost uniformly wanted a more representative form of government. There were mounting calls for a clean break – *ruptura* – by the illegal opposition parties. After the assassination of Admiral Luis Carrero Blanco – Franco's choice of a successor – by the Basques, Carlos Arias Navarro was reluctantly confirmed as Prime Minister in 1973 by King Juan Carlos. Close to Franco for some time, Juan Carlos ascended to the Spanish throne, instead of his father Don Juan – Alfonso XIII's son – and during several critical moments in the eventual transition to democracy, he stepped out of Franco's shadow, earning the respect and affection of the Spanish people.[82] By 1976, Arias had ushered in a limited program of reforms, as violence erupted and continued in the streets, before resigning. He was succeeded by Adolfo Suárez, who, contrary to many predictions, for he came from the Moviemiento Nacional and a conservative Catholic background, moved quickly to introduce a sweeping political reform bill, stunning many of the old regime. Later in the year, the bill was overwhelmingly endorsed by Parliament and by a public referendum to the tune of 94.2 percent in favor. During the subsequent elections called for in the bill, Suárez remained as Prime Minister, having joined the Unión de Centro Democrático (UCD), which gained 34 percent of the vote, followed by the Partido Socialista Obrero Español (PSOE) led by Felipe González, with 29 percent of the vote and with the Allianza Popular (AP) on the right, and the Spanish Communist Party (PCE) on the far left, making relatively poor showings.[83] Clearly Spain had voted for political moderation in contrast to the divisiveness of the past. Finally, in 1978 a new constitution – the eleventh since the beginning of the century – was passed. Considered otherwise very liberal by European standards, it defined Spain as a parliamentary monarchy and has stood the nation in good stead ever since. After 37 years of dictatorial rule, however, not to mention the other setbacks and spasmodic movements of reprieve, that characterized Barcelona's fortunes since the glory days of the *fin de siècle* and early twentieth century, the city was now looking dilapidated, dusty and down at heal. Indeed, on his first visit to the city, during the early 1970s, this author was reminded of the haphazard and careless circumstances of Latin American towns and cities. Apart from surface appearances, Barcelona was an overly-dense place, trading on spatially consolidated property values, and referred to locally as 'the second densest city in the world after Calcutta.' Many areas also lacked schools, recreational open spaces, as well as other public services, and the quality of building construction was often shoddy and low. Although much had changed, the city's plight in these regards, not to mention immigration and political suppression, offered parallels to the time before the city walls came down.

HOLDING THE LINE .... *'in spirit and form, and not forlorn.'*

Passeig de Gràcia

Passeig de Gràcia

Passeig de Gràcia

Passeig de Gràcia

Xamfrans in the Eixample

Xamfrans in the Eixample

Avinguda Diagonal towards Poblenou

L'Illa

Plaça Catalunya

Corte Inglés

TRANSITIONS .... *'moving on up on the east side'*

Barracas at Somorrostro, 1966

Somorrostro

Polígon de la Mina, 1973

Carrer d'Albània

Carrer d'Albània

Diagonal Mar

COLLECTIVE POSSESSION

Simply put, a collective possession is something that everyone owns, has an interest in, or identifies with in some manner. These senses of possession can vary from co-incident private concerns, to a mutuality of use and appreciation, to common cause and outright embrace of public good. Moreover, identity usually comes by way of a common notion of representiveness and a sense of pride. In the case of a city, reference to it as a collective possession involves shared affinities with what's either in place or might be in place, together with a convergence of interests, as numerous individuals, institutions and other entities find something in common, usually involving both the state and civil society. Denied ready access to one of the key ingredients of civil society during the Franco period, various interests in Barcelona muddled along with a mixture of passive acceptance, covert behavior and mounting resistance. Although there was a conspicuous absence of a public sphere where citizens could engage openly in public activities and debate on matters of public interest, both among themselves and with the state, by the late 1960s and early 1970s social movements had formed, each more or less concerned with the deteriorated plight of their city. Two issue that united many were poor living conditions and a lack of public services. Another was the age-old desire for respect, identity and even autonomy within the broader Spanish scheme of things. Present as a subject in many discussions was the stuff, fabric and physical aspect of the city itself and how to 'take it back,' so to speak, and make it more livable and the product of local cultural enterprise.

Taking Back the City

The first major effort to take Barcelona back actually began before Franco's death and involved the pressing need, at least on the part of some, for a workable metropolitan plan. No such instrument had really existed since the 1953 Regional or County Plan and the pattern of urban growth, as well as related social and environmental conditions had changed appreciably since then, as discussed in the last chapter. The Directive Plan of 1968, although producing useful analytical studies and insights that could be built upon, was not officially recognized. It also covered a broad regional geography, encapsulating 162 municipalities including Barcelona, with land-use abstractions and infrastructural proposals that provided little specific guidance, especially in those areas of the city that were developing in a concentrated fashion.[1] Under these circumstances Joan Antoni Solans – the Head of Urban Planning for the Corporació Metropolitana de Barcelona formed at the outset – together with Manuel de Solà-Morales, embarked upon revisions to the 1953 Regional Plan, beginning in 1974, although de Solà-Morales became sidelined along the way. After considerable study and negotiation with interest groups around the city, the General Metropolitan Plan emerged and was approved in 1976. Reasons for its relatively swift enactment included the dire need to put urban controls and service plans in place, something of a power vacuum at the height of political transition in Spain, an embrace of many local-area demands, a period of economic crisis, and the helping hands of the earlier resistance movements. As Solans remarked later, "there was really no other alternative."[2] Not insignificantly, the completed plan was later implemented, at least in part, by Mayor Enric Massó – an industrialist and transitional political figure – who took a different attitude to Barcelona than Porcioles his predecessor. Indeed, by then Solans was serving as his planning director in city hall.

Basically the 1976 General Metropolitan Plan provided a new legal framework for tackling the large volume of demands and conflicts that had accumulated over the years. The watchwords of the plan were 'reconstruction and harmonization of urban space,' as it focused on improvement and restructuring of Barcelona, rather than on extension. Abandoning belief in the creation of a document that would precipitate an 'open process,' as happened with the 1953 Plan's provision for free reign on urban development activity, the planners of the 1976 Plan opted for a mechanism to facilitate rebalancing and control of urbanization.[3] For them, the main issue was tangible reconstruction of the city and, although timidly, they pointed towards the general idea of 'projects not plans,' that was to begin to unfold with full vigor later in the 1980s. Conceptually, the General Metropolitan Plan borrowed heavily from Italian planning processes of the 1960s with a strong Milanese influence, and specifically from Edoardo Detti's plan for Florence and Giuseppe Sanmonna's plan for Rome.[4] Narrower in geographic scope than the 1968 Directive Plan, Solan's plan focused on Barcelona and the 26 surrounding municipalities that constituted the Corporación Metropolitana de Barcelona. Within this focus, building density was radically reconsidered, resulting in something on the order of 27 to 30 percent less density than was allowed during the prior speculative era.[5] Put another way, before the 1976 General Metropolitan Plan, the area within the Corporación Metropolitana de Barcelona could legally allow a population of nine million inhabitants. This was cut back by about 50 percent, to around 4.5 million. In fact, the Municipality of Barcelona's actual population peaked, between 1975 and 1980 at 1.75 million people, with roughly the same population in the surrounding municipalities. Among other issues, the logic behind this legal de-densification of Barcelona, with consensus from the City Council, was the need to relieve traffic congestion and the need to provide adequate space for parks and other public facilities. Indeed, to make up for the lack of services, some 3,000 million pesetas were spent by the municipal government, during a two-year transition period between 1976 and 1978, in order to acquire land in the form of disused industrial property and the last remaining large estates, to be set aside for parks, schools and other public facilities. In total some 86 hectares was acquired for parks and public gardens, 50 hectares for forestry, and 15 hectares for housing and urban rehabilitation.[6]

Technically, the General Metropolitan Plan was an emergency plan of sorts, incorporating a mixture of proposals and methods.[7] At the time of its formulation, there were two competing views about planning. One was to follow the Anglo-American-style 'structural plans,' whereby a metropolis was seen essentially through unifying, usually large-scale infrastructure improvements, like roads and public facilities, with remaining and adjacent property to be left up to market forces and later specification. The other viewpoint was that the plan should control as much development as possible, largely in response to the urban disarray and inefficiency brought on by the sum of many past, small-scale speculative violations. From this latter perspective, which largely prevailed, a 'structural plan' would be quickly outstripped by indiscriminate development, whereas a city seen as an 'architecture of parts,' at least in Barcelona's case, was more likely to match requisite demands for reconstruction, upgrading and improvement of public spaces. In service of this view, a novel zonal division of urban areas was worked up, based upon the architectural typology of each area and its use, although not entirely as a strict morpho-typological plan. A classification system was also devised, which co-incided with traditional land-use classes, enabling land with particular community interests at stake to be taken off the market (i.e., as property not for development), alongside of clear definition of property that could be developed.[8] Although simple, this scheme had the virtue of precision and clarity and was specially devised to prevent the Plan from falling prey to the sort of political-speculative gerrymandering that had gone on in the past. Elsewhere, the General Metropolitan Plan recommended a system of roads, that was inherited largely from the highway network nurtured by the Ministry of Public Works, as well as a program of motorways spread out in order to maximize uses of land for pressing larger-scale projects.

On par, the General Metropolitan Plan proved to be successful. Its implementation put the brakes on deterioration of many parts of Barcelona and stopped the crippling process of densification, no doubt to the chagrin of property speculators used to the concentration of potential financial value in the most built-up parts of the city. It also allowed reclamation of spaces for public use for the citizens of Barcelona and, in so doing, established a suitable framework for later democratic running of the city, by opening the way for later special plans and projects that were tangible to local users. Indeed, in these regards, the General Metropolitan Plan placed Barcelona ahead of other Spanish cities, whose first democratic councils had to scramble in the face of new demands, often having to issue denials of development until suitable plans were put in place. The land bought up for future public use also proved to be very popular, at least in concept, and as a way of gaining support from local citizen groups.

Among the groups who largely defended the General Metropolitan Plan, while also offering a fair share of criticism, were the neighborhood associations. These local citizen groups began forming around the early 1970s in response to poor and deteriorating living conditions in many areas, a lack of services and public open space, a high incidence of crime, a lack of school facilities and poor quality schools, as well as poor building quality and construction.[9] Needless to say, these neighborhood associations also offered a degree of resistance against the Franco regime and were often organized by anti-Franco 'grass roots' district committees, that set about to take inventory and analyze local living conditions as a basis for rallying people together and to face their local problems with a united front. The associations were, *de jure*, legal within prevailing legislation that allowed for the existence of district level social centers, in spite of an otherwise paucity of civil and social liberties. Mayor Massó was also receptive to neighborhood associations because, for him, they opened up a more direct channel between local constituencies and the Ajuntament. One aspect of the General Metropolitan Plan that particularly disturbed neighborhood associations was the provision of special urban planning areas – *Plans Parcials* – promoted by property speculators and developers, because they were seen to deny access for popular local proposals. The Federation of Neighborhood Associations was also formed among some thirty populist local districts, providing an even more concerted voice for the neighborhood movement.[10] Denied access to the usual range of media, they communicated through local bulletins and neighborhood papers. The Assemblea de Catalunya, a unification of particularly clandestine leftists, which formed in 1971, also provided an organ for discussion, debate and communication. Largely, the Assemblea was an outgrowth of the Permanent Assembly of Catalan Intellectuals that was created in 1970 around the protest of the execution of six members of ETA – *Euskadi Ta Askatasuna* – the Basque separist movement, stemming from the infamous Borgos trial.

On many fronts, the period of the late 1960s through to the political transition in the mid-1970s, was increasingly turbulent in Barcelona. There were numerous demonstrations, political sloganeering, strikes and confrontations with the police. One of the first institutions to become politicized was the university. In 1966, some 69 professors were suspended for several years because of their political tendencies and, by January of 1969 a 'state of emergency' was declared by Franco's government in the face of the mounting student revolution. Mass demonstrations in Barcelona's more prominent public spaces and in its streets led to indiscriminate repression and arrests, including numerous members of PSUC – the Unified Socialist Party of Catalonia – students, leftist professors and progressive Catholics. Then in 1970, 143 professionals, intellectuals and staff of the university wrote an open letter to the central government demanding democracy. As more and more students became involved in politics, unrest in the university escalated, also involving numerous intellectuals, artists, and other prominent public figures.[11] The church also became politicized and split along generational lines, particularly by the Second Vatican Council in the mid-1960s, leading, in 1966, to a Spanish law liberalizing worship in credos other than Roman Catholic. The progressive Catholic intelligentsia also offered fierce resistance to the ultraconservative and shadowy Opus Dei and many among the clergy provided support and facilitation for clandestine social movements, as well as support for regional nationalism.[12] Trade unions, illegal during Franco's time, nevertheless became increasingly well organized, precipitating strikes and other resistive political activities.

Over much the same time, Barcelona also became a haven for prominent Latin American writers – the so-called Grupo de Barcelona. This group included Gabriel García Márquez from Columbia, who arrived in the late 1960s; Mario Vargas Llosa from Peru, also stayed there during the early 1970s; and Julio Cortázar, the Argentinean, who sojourned intermittently up through the early 1980s.[13] Their cultural impact was not insubstantial and, although not involved in the resistance and transition to the same extent as the locals, their presence added further to the calls for change and the emergence of Barcelona as not another passive and parochial Spanish town. Finally, in 1975 the Catalan Lawyers Collegiate also made open demands for a democracy, a Catalan government, and amnesty for political prisoners. As several other authors have observed, the active emergence of these and other elements of civil society probably hastened the steps towards democracy and made the movement that much more comprehensive.[14] Following the election called for in Suárez's reform bill at the national level, the Generalitat was re-established in Barcelona, in September of 1977, with, as mentioned earlier, Josep Tarradellas, now returned from exile, as its President.

After the sweeping passage of the new Spanish constitution, the first cycle of regular general elections took place at both the national and municipal level. Adolfo Suárez maintained his premiership of Spain, with the centrist UCD gaining 168 seats, or 48 percent, in the legislature, followed by the socialist PSOE with 121 seats, or 35 percent.[15] These were improvements for both parties over their showings in 1977, signaling the beginning of a consolidation of the Spanish electorate into two broad camps, to the left and right of the political spectrum. By 1980, however, discussion in the ranks of the UCD began to erupt between the liberals and those on the far right, together with traditionalists content to tinker with Franco's political legacy, over domestic issues like divorce and abortion rights. In 1981, Suárez resigned, joining the liberal faction, and he was replaced by Leopoldo Calvo Sotelo.[16] During the same year, there was a threat to the fledgling democracy, in the form of an attempted military coup, when a Civil Guard contingent held the *Cortes* hostage at gunpoint for a period of about 24 hours, only to be thwarted by Juan Carlos' timely and deft handling of the situation. With the subsequent general election in 1982, Spain settled down into its contemporary pattern of parties and party politics to the left and right of the political aisle. The election was won handsomely by the PSOE, with an absolute majority of 202 seats, ably led by Felipe González. For some time González had been dragging his socialist party towards the center on a platform of liberal economics and modern governance, realizing correctly that the fulcrum of Spanish politics lay somewhere around the center left. To the right, the AP emerged as the major opposition party, with 106 seats, and the UCD virtually became disbanded, as the Social Democrats joined the PSOE and the Christian Democrats linked up with the AP.

Results of the 1979 election in Barcelona and the 1980 election in Catalonia somewhat mirrored those at the national level, but with their own local twists. Instead of the center right, the PSC – *Partit dels Socialistes de Catalunya* – in alliance with others on the left, took over the municipal government under the leadership of Narcís Serra, whereas Jordi Pujol – of the *Convergència i Uni* or Convergence and Union Party – took over the regional government, by presenting a populist alternative to those on the left, including a mixture of tempered Catalan nationalism and bourgeoisie middle-class values.[17] Indeed, until very recently and Pujol's retirement from active politics, this voting pattern continued, exhibiting a certain *seny* or 'hedging of bets' on the part of the electorates. Clearly, close to home in Barcelona, the socialists were the most trusted to deliver good government and services, while further abroad in the region, the more conservative Catalan nationalists were favored, especially as a counter-weight to centralizing tendencies in Madrid.

It also has to be said that the political valence of Catalonia, beyond Barcelona, was more towards the right anyway. Nevertheless, a formula was struck across the Plaça Sant Jaume – the home of both the Ajuntament and the Generalitat – whereby Catalan pride and a sense of identity could flower once more, alongside of socially-conscious and able administration that reached out to the local populace. In both orientation and action, Serra's socialists were a new breed who were largely upbeat and ambitious for their city and devoid of hide-bound and dour views typical of the left in other parts of Europe, such as in Italy. Serra, for his part is an economist, who graduated from Barcelona's School of Economic Sciences in 1973 with a Ph.D., later becoming appointed as an Honorary Fellow of the London School of Economics in 1991. Between 1966 and 2000, he served as a general secretary of the earlier clandestine PSC and was Secretary of Defense in González's Spanish Government, between 1982 and 1991; followed by the Vice Presidency, between 1991 and 1995.[18]

Pujol, by contrast, has stayed closer to home. Although he studied medicine, he became well known in his early years as the creator of the Catalan Bank in 1959. An activist against Franco, Pujol spent three years in jail for his efforts during the 1960s and was a founder of the Convergència Democràtica de Catalunya. Before becoming leader of the CiU, he served as an advisor to the Generalitat under Tarradellas.[19] A charismatic character with broad popular appeal, particularly among land owners, the middle classes and upper-working class, Pujol was also a reformist in his own inimitable way.

By 1983 and 1984, respectively, for the municipality and the region, the political cast, as for the nation, was even more strongly set around the center to both the left and the right. At the municipal level, led now by Pasqual Maragall, Serra's former deputy and council officer for organization and reform, the PSC won 45 percent of the vote, to the CiU's 27 percent, whereas almost the reverse occurred at the regional level, with Pujol's CiU gaining 47 percent to the PSC's 30 percent.[20] Maragall is also an economist, receiving his Ph.D. from the Universitat Autònoma de Barcelona, where he also taught, as well as a lawyer. Active in promoting urban causes outside of Barcelona, Maragall founded Eurocities in 1989, chaired the first Conference of Mediterranean Cities in 1995 and served as President of the European Union's Committee of Regions in 1996, among other active involvements. Like Pujol, he has participated at the forefront of Barcelona's and Catalonia's political scene for most of his professional life, although from the left.[21]

While democracy and the institutions that go with it were being established in Barcelona, there was something of a lull in broader cultural activity. Gone were most members of the lively ex-patriot Grupo de Barcelona, as already noted, and little activity of note was occurring in theater, opera, film or fine arts. In a reference to the 'Titanic,' gaily sailing along into the jaws of disaster, Félix de Azúa, a local writer, declared in a pungent *El País* article in 1982, that "nothing is happening in Barcelona" and that "everything is taking place in Madrid." He even went on to refer to some artists and intellectuals, who rented a bus to travel to Madrid in order to view an exhibition of a Catalan artist, such was the difference in the cultural and intellectual ambiance of the two cities.[22] Azúa was also not alone in his critique of local circumstances, striking a resonant chord, when he called for more substantial investment on culture by both the Ajuntament and the Generalitat. Without taking anything away from Azúa, or like-minded members of the intelligentsia, these circumstances were perhaps understandable, given the sheer effort required, especially by those in government, to exact necessary reforms and to get things moving. In this respect, again there is a parallel with the lull that occurred after the murallas were removed and Cerdà's plan was adopted during the mid-nineteenth century, as noted in chapter one. This was also a time when Spain's economy went into recession, sinking from a healthy 4 percent year-on-year rise in GDP to around zero, between 1977 and 1981, with inflation spiraling close to 25 percent. Nevertheless, as the well-known author Eduardo Mendoza remarked later, again with reference to Azúa's 'Titanic' analogy, that Barcelona was like a "big boat, well built but going down. It was time to do something." Moreover, with reference to the void left by the end of Franco's dictatorship, it was "as if we in Barcelona woke up forty years later and had to decide who we were. Mom and dad," so to speak, with a certain irony, "were dead."[23]

Urban Public Space Projects

At least on the urban front, public expenditure and renewal of the city was not long in coming and, in particular, through efforts to accede to popular demand for more open space and to take up the promissories of the 1976 General Metropolitan Plan. Completed between 1981 and 1987, the urban public space projects of

Barcelona represent a large and impressive body of public work at widely different scales, spread throughout the city.[24] The program officially began in December 1980, when Mayor Serra appointed a five-member town planning commission to assess the urban issues confronting the city. The members were: Josep-Miguel Abad, the vice mayor; Oriol Bohigas, a legislative delegate and, since 1979, head of planning; Jaume Galofré, a lawyer; Albert Puigdomènech, a planner; and Josep-Anton Acebillo, an architect. After examining the General Metropolitan Plan of 1976, the commission strongly recommended the immediate development of highly specific and much needed open-space projects, both to quickly and relatively inexpensively establish a strong public presence and to help renovate the city. In addition, the commission recommended general adoption of the 1976 General Metropolitan Plan, although largely as a medium-term reference tool and, as originally intended, a normative device covering property transactions among businesses and the general populace within the city. By favoring adoption of a program of specific projects, the commission clearly recognized that the urban space needs of Barcelona were relatively well known and nothing would be gained from pursuing the abstractions of further master planning exercises. In these regards, the commission was also following up on the demands of neighborhood associations and opportunities provided by the 'land bank' accrued in connection with Solans' and other's efforts during the mid-1970s. Moreover, the underlying rationale was much the same as that expressed in the 1976 General Metropolitan Plan and, for that matter, the much earlier Cerdà plan, namely the improvement of public health and alleviation of poorly serviced and overcrowded living conditions.

Under the direction of Acebillo, a special urban design team was formed in 1981 at the Ajuntament, known as the Office of Urban Projects, which later became decentralized.[25] The first commissions were then quickly conceived and constructed. During the early stages, all public improvements were confined to the project sites themselves, and there were little to no displacements of population or viable urban functions from surrounding areas. Furthermore, projects were undertaken in all ten districts within Barcelona: Ciutat Vella, Eixample, Sants-Montjuïc, Les Corts, Sarrià- Sant Gervasi, Gràcia, Horta-Guinardó, Nous Barris, Sant Andreu, and Sant Martí. This was to be a program for the entire city, but one that would eventually operate in a home-grown decentralized manner, fitting the needs of particular geographic locales and groups regardless of their socioeconomic and physical circumstances. Apart from being a local jurisdiction, each district also corresponded to a distinctive area within the city, already partly recognized in the 1976 General Metropolitan Plan, that warranted special urban design considerations. Gràcia, for instance, like several other districts as noted earlier, was once a small town on the outskirts of Barcelona, which eventually became engulfed by urban development during the nineteenth and early twentieth centuries, as Barcelona made its way north from the sea to the hills. Gràcia has an irregular arrangement of small streets and modest-sized buildings for which small paved plazas and pedestrial areas, in the Mediterranean tradition, are most appropriate. Sants-Monjuïc, by contrast, is more open and diverse in its physical conformation, thus warranting larger-scaled open-space projects. Almost from the beginning, design personnel within the Office of Urban Projects were assigned specifically to each district to become familiar with local needs and to work with citizens, businesses, and other interest groups.

In addition to the Office of Urban Projects, numerous other designers, particularly young architects, again like earlier times and particularly in conjunction with the First Universal Exhibition of 1888, were commissioned to carry out projects. In 1983 Maragall also enthusiastically embraced the urban space program and continued to expand its influence. Joan Busquets, a faculty member of the University of Barcelona, also joined the City Hall staff at this time in a supervisory role as head of planning and infrastructure. By 1987, when Barcelona began to focus its attention elsewhere, more than 100 urban space projects had been completed, beginning with small-scaled urban plazas and ending with extensive improvements to the Moll de la Fusta along Barcelona's waterfront, the first installment of the Rondas. Today the number of completed projects stands well in excess of 150, as each of the separate districts undertakes its own projects, following the lead of the earlier public works program. Attention then turned toward other sorts of related public improvements in housing, schools and transportation.

Three kinds of urban public space projects – plazas, parks, and streets – were completed under the initial program. Some, such as the Plaça Real and the Parc Güell, were renovations and restorations of existing urban places, whereas many of the others, such as Plaça dels Països Catalans and the nearby Parc de l'Espanya Industrial, were new improvements within the city. Some plazas, such as the Plaça de la Mercè to be found in Ciutat Vella, as well as those found in the district of Gràcia, were relatively small, discreet and hard surfaced. Others, like the Plaça dels Països Catalans, or Sants Plaza, were far more extensive with more dynamic boundary conditions, although equally hard surfaced. Neighborhood parks, such as the Parc del Clot and the Plaça de la Palmera, contain a variety of recreational activities, as well as public artworks by major international artists like Bryan Hunt and Richard Serra.[26] In the Plaça de la Palmera, for instance, Serra's curving walls are an integral part of the park's life, creatively dividing serene, well-planted, and contemplative spaces from the active terrain of youngsters' games. Other parks, such as the Parc de Joan Miró, on a site formerly occupied by a slaughterhouse, are more extensive and were intended for citywide use. Here, varied settings of well-planted areas, open plazas, and sports facilities are found within a single site. Street projects such as the Avinguda de Gaudí focusing on the Sagrada Família, and the multi-level Via Júlia – the main street of a low-income neighborhood on the outskirts of Barcelona – have created well-appointed pedestrian environments where only vehicular traffic congestion and dilapidated storefronts once existed. Others, such as the early Passeig de Picasso, provide straightforward definition and pedestrian relief on heavily traveled streets, whereas the Moll de Bosch i Alsina, or Moll de la Fusta, extending along much of the city's harbor front, is both a park and a street system combined, simultaneously rerouting traffic, providing a public face to the city, and accommodating leisure-time activities.

Throughout the urban space program, a shared intellectual idea of Barcelona accompanied the strong conviction that the city was in large part something tangible, objective, and capable of renewal. Given this common agenda, however, there was also a tolerance of formal design diversity reminiscent of other moments of Catalan modernism, such as the earlier periods of Gaudí, Domènech i Montaner, Puig i Cadafalch, or of Sert, described in chapter one. Among the contemporary projects, this diversity extended from the minimalism of the Plaça del Països Catalans, by Piñón and Viaplana, to the expressionistic contexturalism of the Parc de l'Espanya Industrial, by Peña Ganchegui and Rius, as well as more prosaically from softly planted surfaces to the traditionally hard-paved plazas. In the final analysis, a broadly-based and authentic Catalan style of place making emerged.

Most of these shared intellectual ideas centered around the Barcelona School of Architecture during the 1970s, and teachers such as Manuel de Solà-Morales, author of the Moll de al Fusta and founder of the Laboratori d'Urbanisme; Rafael Moneo; and particularly the head of the School of Architecture at the time, Oriol Bohigas. Throughout the school, and in special units, such as the Laboratori d'Urbanisme, the city became a preoccupation. No project rose above the city in importance, and all contributed to what became a shared urban idea. Central to this idea was the perception of Barcelona as an aggregation of different and distinctive quarters or districts, as noted earlier, rather than as a general system of functions. Considerable emphasis was also placed on continuing the significance of the city's traditional morphology, but in new urban-architectural ways, and on a shared regional past of considerable architectural merit. Through a process that Bohigas likened to *metastasis*, local projects were to be deployed as catalyst for upgrading the overall quality of the city.[27] Thus the value of public improvements could be leveraged substantially and the interaction between elements of the government and civil society stimulated accordingly.

Also underlying Barcelona's open-space program was a strong commitment to diversity in the social arrangement and expression of projects. Indeed, physical and expressive variety among local projects, once broad norms and intentions had been established, was seen as a matter of both progress and survival. In these regards the urban public spaces of Barcelona embraced a broad range of functions, with many of the parks equipped for specific recreational and leisure-time activities. The architects and public officials were keenly aware of the plurality of interests confronting them as various groups in civil society began to assert themselves. The Parc de l'Escorxador or Parc de Joan Miró, by Antoni Solanas in conjunction with the Office of Urban Projects, for example, provided facilities for organized basketball and football games within its expansive landscape. Less formal but nevertheless significant venues were also established, within a garden setting on the same site, for other organized recreational pursuits such as bowling. By contrast, many of the small plazas within the city, such as those in Gràcia and within Ciutat Vella, simply provided the opportunity for respite from the bustle of daily city life and were far less programmatically specific. More often than not, these paved spaces provide outdoor public 'rooms,' as it were, within the otherwise private realm of the city and are conformed to enhance the surrounding architecture. The small plaza alongside the venerable Santa Maria del Mar, the Fossar de les Moreres by Carme Fiol – for instance, admirably achieved both civic purposes, while serving in it own right to memorialize the Catalan martyrs of 1714. In addition, considerable emphasis was placed on multiple uses of public spaces. Almost all in some way accommodated the daily rituals of meeting, strolling, and simply being together in a public place – all strong cultural characteristics of Barcelona's life. Indeed, among various parks, plazas, and streets, these straightforward yet crucial activities were provided for amply. Many, including the Plaça de la Mercè and the Plaça Reial, for instance, also now accommodate and were designed for more formal collective gatherings of commemoration, political expression and celebration.

Two other related aspects of this functional and formal diversity also deserve special note. First, throughout the urban public space program, an inventive and productive awareness was apparent concerning differences between various open-space functions and the degree to which those differences should be reflected in design. Sometimes, unfortunately, the formal variation of urban space, in general, can be accomplished too readily for its own sake, rather than as a reflection of vital cultural interests. Conversely, social diversity can be denied, in principle, through an overly monolithic insistence on a particular style or approach. Fortunately, in Barcelona a sensitive awareness of appropriate design difference in various links of the roadway network, for example, is spatially very apparent. Here one immediately confronts essential differences among streets for traffic, avenues that accommodate both traffic and people strolling, and the *passeig*, which accommodates both activities and yet has a higher-order civic role to perform as a gathering place. Within the physical realm of Barcelona, for example, the new versions of the Avinguda de Gaudí, the Passeig Colom, and the Passeig de Picasso can hardly be confused, although on the city plan they may all appear to be nothing more than major roadway segments.

The second important aspect of formal and functional diversity was realization of an appropriate level of indeterminacy in design. Once again, a proposal can be so specific as to rule out reappropriation of public spaces for other desirable yet unforeseen uses, or designs can be so vague and bereft of ideas about use that they become alienating and intimidating. Fortunately, in places like the Parc de l'Espanya Industrial by Luis Peña Ganchegui and Rius, for example, the stepped inclined edge that forms an exuberant backdrop to the park itself is routinely used by spectators at outdoor events as well as by a plethora of more informal users for sunbathing, reading, lounging, or simply socializing. Similarly, the surfaces of the Avinguda de Gaudí, by Màrius Quintana, are a haven for skateboard riders, hopscotch enthusiasts, street vendors, strollers, and delivery men on lunch breaks. Likewise, the Via Júlia clearly demonstrates that the traditional repertoire of streets can be cleverly rejuvenated to accommodate many modern exigencies of both transit and repose. Large portions of Via Júlia, for instance, are nonspecialized areas, allowing for a considerable amount of local invention to occur. The trellis area above the subway station, partially buried beneath the project, contains a large sitting area for afternoon conversation, a market held at least once a week, and a festival site or area for community gathering and public functions. Dominated by a large lantern tower that marks its intersection with the adjacent high-speed ring road, the Via Júlia has become both a *rambla* and a center of neighborhood activity in a dense, low-income area of the city as well as an armature from which other public open spaces now extend.

For a process of urban refurbishing and remaking to take hold among an urban populace and to become adopted as a fundamental part of a new image for the city, regardless of pent-up demands, those in government must find the right level at which decision making matters most. In urban design, this invariably means identifying the scale at which there is sufficient congruence between city form, social purpose, and cultural values to make a palpable difference in the daily life of citizens. Unfortunately, such decisions often vary between the abstractions of plan making and broad social programs that attempt to satisfy everyone and yet often end up enfranchising very few, and the construction of favored local projects that have become the pet causes of powerful interest groups. Fortunately in this instance, the city of Barcelona avoided the pitfalls of both positions.

From a social perspective the urban public spaces program addressed one of the city's most pressing problems – namely the need for viable open spaces within what was a dense urban fabric of buildings. Whether it was in fact the most pressing need could be argued, although an obvious competing issue like housing appeared to be more one of distribution than of sheer insufficiency and it was addressed later anyway. From a political perspective, the program offered the important potential of relatively quick, prominent, and tangible results from public investment. Furthermore, the relative cost-effectiveness was high, far less expensive than schools, for example, another deficient use within the city. This allowed projects to be distributed throughout the city, leaving few of its citizens unaffected. Even large improvements, such as the Plaça dels Països Catalans and the city-wide parks, were relatively inexpensive to construct, and the effect of the design results on urban space users was almost instantaneous.

Along with the creation of an appropriate vehicle for making public improvements, however, comes the need for strong political will and vision. On both counts it is clear that the local government administration was formed and aggressively led by Mayors Serra and Maragall. Not only did they enthusiastically endorse the urban public spaces program, even during times of controversy, but both men also had an unusual tolerance for experimentation. Narcís Serra, for example, was directly responsible for the prolific installation of contemporary public art, traveling to New York, for instance, to interest American artists in participating. However, without diminishing the central role of public officials, an interest in novelty and experimentation can partly be explained by the larger historical circumstances of the urban space program. For some time during the Franco regime, very little renovation had occurred in Barcelona and the democratic elections of 1979 signaled a strong break with the past. Under these circumstances it is little wonder that a return to traditional approaches would be eschewed in favor of confidently striking out in a new contemporary direction much as happened during the *fin de siècle*, almost a century ago. Moreover, technically speaking, no adequate indigenous precedents existed for many of the contemporary spatial conditions that had to be resolved. Thus in most cases, invention was the only recourse.

One of the most noteworthy innovations was the extensive use of hard paved and masonry surfaces, the *plaça dura*. Although controversial, particularly when expressed on the vast scale of the Plaça dels Països Catalans, there were several reasons behind this rather consistent choice of surface for public open spaces. First, immediate and pragmatic use could be made of available materials and an available craft tradition, which obvious cost and socioeconomic benefits. Second, the hard surfaces were durable, relatively easy to maintain, and symbolically gave an immediate appearance of project completion. Third, a broader culturally-based decision was made that Barcelona belonged to the tradition of no trees, rather than vice versa. Among the intelligentsia of the design community at the time there was a preference for hard urban plazas in a Mediterranean tradition, such as those found in Italy, and skepticism expressed about the image of abundant trees and lawns in the presentation of an emphatically public plaza.

In keeping with other broad themes of the urban space program, this new tradition also allowed for considerable expressive variety among separate projects, partly promoted by specific design circumstances. The Plaça Reial, by Federico Correa and Alfonso Milá, for instance, concerned the restoration of the original plaza created by royal decree beside the Rambla and originally designed in 1848, as mentioned in chapter one, by Francesco Daniel Molina. Incorporating several civic monuments, the plaza was paved throughout, with furnishings forming an inner plaza parallel with the surrounding building facades. Tall palm trees were planted at regular intervals, conforming in plan to a complex axial arrangement. Unlike the original, however, the entire plaza can now be comprehended immediately as a singular spatial entity. Similarly, the nearby neoclassical Plaça de la Mercè, by the Office of Urban Projects, is a renovated space. Modestly understated and civic in outlook, the plaza is paved simply, with a fountain and a nineteenth-century sculpture found in a nearby warehouse serving as a central focus. Finally, the controversial Plaça dels Països Catalans, by Heli Piñón and Albert Viaplana, was also a new installation, although unprecedented, as noted earlier, in its minimalist expression. Formerly the site of a large parking lot in front of Barcelona's major commuter rail station, the new plaza was designed to avoid interfering with surrounding traffic systems, including the rail lines underneath. Under these conditions the paved surface and skeletal structures are understandable, yet the result accomplishes far more than a basic material utility. The dynamic formal abstractions of frames, bollards, benches, and light stanchions bring order to an otherwise vast and disparate space in an extraordinary parsimonious manner. The result is at once functional – providing shade, places to pause, and a certain definition for pedestrian traffic – yet sculpturally engaging, drawing attention to the material conditions surrounding its genesis and the capacity of frames in a field to articulate, effectively command, and volumetrically define the space.

Another noteworthy innovation of Barcelona's urban spaces program was the emergence of a regionally distinctive type of park, involving a strong sense of enframement that simultaneously distinguished the park for surrounding areas and provided for an expressive autonomy within the frame itself. In planimetric terms, it resembled a carefully framed painting on which various overlays were rendered, and in almost all cases where the contrast between hard and soft surfaces, between water bodies and land, and between sculptural installations and their field, were often accentuated. Moreover, one geometric order, such as the planting of trees, was overlaid on another, such as systems of pathways, so that differences between the two orders remained intact rather than being resolved into a third. This process further gave the effected areas of the parks a heightened abstract, three-dimensional quality that they might otherwise have lacked. Specific elements within the overall composition tended to be finite and discontinuous, serving as accents and foci within the normally ordered field of the park. Invariably, one or more of the boundaries took on an irregular, organic shape in stark contrast to the orthogonal and linear forms of surrounding features. In fact, this emerging genre of modern park has become perhaps even more distinctive in Barcelona than the better-known plaça dura.[28]

Less abstractly, in the Parc del Clot, by Daniel Freixes and Vicente Miranda, for instance, enframement was delivered by retaining the outside masonry wall of the large factory structure that formerly occupied the site. A rough division was made on the east side of the park with a bermed, well-planted, and predominantly grassy area, and on the west by a partially sunken paved plaza. Undulations in the ground plane, from the prospect at the top of the berm, provided a singular well-defined sweep of space. The predominant building elements in the composition were bridge structures that literally spanned the berms and paved areas.

Other features, such as an aqueduct-like water body and public art installation by Bryan Hunt, completed the improvements. In another instance, the Parc de l'Espanya Industrial, which also occupies the site of a former factory complex, was carefully enframed by a steeply inclined wall of steps, rising from a sunken area of the site. Again, there is a substantial interplay between soft grassy and well-planted areas. The pervasive imagery of the park, though, differs greatly with the Parc del Clot. It has an idiosyncratic, expressionistic quality, especially in details such as the huge light and observation towers that help define one edge. In addition, both the Parc de la Creueta del Coll, by Martorell, Bohigas, and Mackay in the hills overlooking Barcelona, and the Parc de l'Estació del Nord, by the Office of Urban Projects, with its extraordinary sculptural installation by Beverly Pepper, closer to the center of the city, possess many of the same general spatial features, as does the Vil·la Cecília garden complex by Elías Torres and José Antonio Martínez Lapeña. The Creueta del Coll also seems precendented on the Parc Güell, with its sinuous winding path, building juxtaposed to rock outcropping, and well-made balustrade atop rusticated walls. However, this backward reference, like many others among the public space projects in Barcelona, may be subliminal rather than explicit and coming from a deeper cultural code giving form to design action. The Vil·la Cecília garden also incorporates several other tropes of the public space projects. In addition to the idea of spatial rooms with an overall composition, there is both a condensation and amplification of 'nature' at work in the artificial topography, also shared at Clot, and the maze-like dissolution of immediate context. The gestural scattering of vegetation, present in other projects as well, also gives a sense of the informal qualities of nature but provides for a double-reading, so to speak, by also appearing to be formal in a painterly manner. There, as elsewhere, the project is about form and structure rather than about, say, color and decorative embellishment, as in other genres of gardens.

Unfortunately, problems have been encountered with such definitive design approaches, even with considerable local district participation. Administrative naiveté and oversight, for instance, prevented the allocation of adequate resources for project maintenance, leaving a number of the earlier projects in need of considerable refurbishing and some even in sad disrepair. The piecemeal character of project organization, in the absence of a more coherent local plan, sometimes led to a lack of design coordination. Novelty and experimentation also had their prices. The absence of immediately identifiable furnishings in several parks has been a point of contention with neighboring residents. At the Parc del Clot, for example, banners draped form upper-story windows in surrounding apartment buildings asked, "When will a real play area be built?" Nevertheless, children enthusiastically continue to play, apparently oblivious to distinctions between contemporary and traditional building practices. It was also not the first time nor last time that Barcelona's leaps of civic design came under criticism.[29] As discussed in chapter one, no less an architectural figure than Puig i Cadafalch, for instance, strongly objected to Cerdà's plan for the Eixample as being far too abstract, egalitarian, and uninteresting for Barcelona's needs, preferring instead Rovira's less undifferentiated and hierarchical proposal.

As alluded to earlier, another aspect of the historical circumstances surrounding the urban public spaces program that warrants closer examination is the timing of economic cycles. Until recently and certainly during the early eighties, the immediate post-Franco period was a time of relative economic downturn, during which little private-sector development occurred on any scale, unlike the previous speculative boom. Because of the strong initiatives taken by city government during this lull, public works could regain an exemplary status and be presented as models for action. In fact, the local administration was practically the only investor in urban development at the time. A situation in which the economy was sluggish, therefore, was successfully converted into one of considerable public leadership. Subsequently, when the economic pendulum swung back again in favor of private investment, a new administrative posture of joint public-private participation in urban development was established, with the local government acting from a position of strength and vision that it probably could not have attained without the earlier public works projects. This was certainly apparent during the Olympic Games preparations of the late 1980s, to be discussed in the following chapter, which catapulted Barcelona, although not without further criticism, into another scale of urban improvements, including completion of a ring road, large-scale housing development, and several kilometers of public beach and adjacent park improvements.

Besides the urban public space projects, attention was also turned by the civil authorities to small elements of infrastructure, like the Felip II bridge – Bac de Roda – by Santiago Calatrava, as well as to needed school and recreational facilities. In many instances the school projects were both reflections of their context, like the public space projects, and yet also expressions of geometric and tectonic purity. Both characteristics are evident in Bohigas Matorell and Mackay's Catalonia Public School of 1981 to 1983, located in an uncompromising, largely industrial urban setting, near the Besòs river. The overall building configuration is unitary and compact, with a repetitive structure of concrete porticoes, and a generally austere material treatment like the industrial architecture of the rest of the area.

Likewise, Eduard Bru and Josep Lluís Mateo's La Bastida Professional Training Center of the same period, takes up with the escarpment on which it is located with a low volume of enclosed workshops, giving a monumental appearance not unsuitable for such an expression that was so fundamentally concerned with the surrounding landscape, capped with a two-storey block of classrooms. Jaume Bach and Gabriel Mora's L'Alzina Public School, both respects the geometry of the city block on which it is situated, as well as the adjacent gardens, while also presenting a well-made masonry prismatic volume, whose specific shape was determined in places by the building's internal program. Indeed, although they have received less international attention, the public schools of this period, of which there are many, generally displayed a civic architecture of contemporary modernity. Also high on the local populace's reformatory agenda, as mentioned earlier, schools were far from perfunctory in appearance and, like the urban public spaces, occasions for architectural experimentation in a new way, further reinforcing – through architecture – a strong sense of public commitment towards the regeneration of needed urban services. The La Sagrera Public School, for instance, by Jordi Bosch, Joan Tarrús and Santiago Vires of 1980 to 1983, was prominently located in its urban setting, prismatic in its volumetric appearance like the L'Alzina Public School, and the site of another sculpture by Richard Serra.
Then too, there were housing projects in a not dissimilar key, such as Jordi Garcés and Enric Soria's Pi i Molist apartment complex, along the street by the same name in the north-east area of the city, or Lluís Nadal's Rio de Janeiro apartment complex, nearby the old Sant Andreu railway station.

Affinity with Urban Architecture

As at other times in the past, throughout the recent transitional period into democracy and beyond, the people of Barcelona exhibited an unusual concern and affinity for the urban-architectural character of their city. To be sure, as elsewhere, this concern and affinity came by way of intimate interaction between citizenry and the urban fabric in which they lived. It also produced, however, an active relationship with a cumulative character that was and remains peculiar to Barcelona, both in its derivation and in its intensity. First, renowned most for its architecture, at least on the international scene, this palpable aspect of Barcelona is its most immediate and principal source of pride. Furthermore, the city itself was and still largely remains synonymous with being Catalan. Indeed, many who live beyond Barcelona *per se*, have strong affinity with the city and believe themselves to be citizens. In addition, along with the Catalan language it is the aspect of this citizenship that has been held on to most and probably worked on more, judging from the number of international expositions and similar pretexts that have been developed since the walls came down, to ambitiously further adorn and embellish the physical aspect of the city. Even during less outgoing moments, such as the period under discussion, it seems as if Barcelonians turned first towards the fabric of their city, despite a relative paucity of means, once they had the freedom of opportunity to do so.

Second, one aspect of seny, that prized trait of the Catalans, is industriousness, breeding 'those who make,' so to speak, and a kind of practical entrepreneurship on an immediate scale. As a consequence of their ambition and success, merchants and local industrialists during earlier times required quality space for selling and for displaying their wealth. Craftsmen and tradespeople, in turn, under much the same rubric of 'getting on with it,' rose to the occasion by fashioning elegant town mansions, places of business, and other urban accouterments, often guided by a deep array of local architectural talent. Although not unaware of their place in the broader world outside, these architects, probably at their best, remained slightly out of step with foreign trends and fashions, producing unique projects that turned, instead, more inward than outward culturally, for sources of inspiration and motivation. Indeed, just as the *fin de siècle* architecture stood out as being part of a broader European movement but not quite, so did the much later public urban space projects. Certainly at the time at which they were constructed, many seemed fresh and novel in spatial conception, subsequently re-invigorating the design of public spaces in other parts of the world. Also, as discussed, the coherence that emerged among most of the projects and perhaps especially among the parks, appears to have been more subliminal than pre-rehearsed, or according to a specific design doctrine, indicating the presence of a latent, common cultural awareness and manner of doing things. To be sure, there were preceding discussions, debates and decisions taken with regard to the broad allocation of various types of public space, like the *plaça dura*. Beyond these explicit agreements, however, considerable latitude was allowed and even encouraged with regard to design freedom, and yet sufficient similarities emerged for the projects to be closely identified with Barcelona, *circa* the 1980s. No doubt intuition, another aspect surrounding *seny*, was also at work, as it was conspicuous among *fin de siècle* architects. Without resorting to much by way of broad theoretical frameworks and other intellectual paraphernalia, designers fell back on, or discovered, their own formal devices which, when operating against broadly-shared backgrounds and, for many, youthful experience, led to common and, given the group as a whole, distinctive common design insights. There was, it should be said, a broad understanding and acceptance of the tenents of the Italian Tendenza, particularly with regard to the appropriateness of ideas about type and specific typologies applied on an urban scale. Nevertheless, even the contemporaneous watchwords – 'projects not plans' – were as much commonsensical as theoretical, given the clarity of perceived need and the socio-political circumstances at the time. It has also been suggested that Barcelonians in many walks of life tend to have more of an intuitive rather than imaginative identity. Returning to the merchants and local industrialists for a moment, their enterprises have certainly been big enough to be significant, although also small enough to be encompassed and handled intuitively, or instinctively. It might also be said that this intuition, coupled with practicality – returning to *seny* for a moment longer – as well as with ambition and the idea of making a mark, lead somewhat inevitably in the direction of building and architecture.

On the side of popular reception of architecture within the city, after years of neglect, there was, as discussed, a clear and palpable need for renovation, particularly in the directions that were taken, namely public open space, schools, other public facilities and housing. There was also broad consensus among the population with regard to these needs, as well as strong and, by then, able support from local groups at a district level, that had become well organized during earlier days of resistance. In addition, these physical needs had been the rallying point among the neighborhood associations and other groups against the Franco regime. Moreover, the municipal government was not only in sympathy with many of these local constituencies but many members had either been a part of, or worked among, those constituencies during earlier political movements against Franco's regime. Therefore, it could be said that they were, more or less, 'cut from the same cloth.' Also, a plan – the 1976 General Metropolitan Plan – was already in place, representing at least a clear beginning for re-balancing the physical framework and reconstructuring the city. Fortunately, this planning process had also accrued a significant amount of property within Barcelona into municipal ownership, from which many popular public needs could be addressed in both a timely and cost-effective manner.

Barcelona is also quintessentially a 'street city.' People habitually use the streets and surrounding urban environments for many aspects of their daily lives, take to the streets at moments of demonstration and revolt, and make use of public space as a sphere of emancipatory appearance. Consequently, Barcelonians are constantly in touch with the physical aspect of their city, its monuments, places of gathering, promenades and quieter corners of respite. Rather than bland anthropological usage, there is also a curious and critical sense in which they take possession of their public realm. Even during times when the city was disrupted and partially dismembered by construction projects, people appeared happy, paying visits to the public works, expressing opinions like "this is going well, but I would do something more over here," and so on. Certainly, during the 1980s every proposal seemed to be well entertained and taken on eagerly. Moreover, as Mendoza again once commented, "everyone sees themselves as a potential architect."[30] In addition, another reason for being a 'street city,' certainly at the time under discussion, was that living space in dwellings was often small, thwart with inter-generational living, and overcrowded. To go out in the city was more comfortable and also brought a heightened sense of common property and, therefore, interest in what was and was not being constructed. For women, in particular, appearance in the public realm, rather than staying at home, as earlier tradition would have required, further reinforced their growing sense of emancipation in Barcelona and the new Spain.

Finally, Barcelona, even at around 1.7 million inhabitants, was a compact city, mainly sandwiched between the mountains and the sea and the two rivers – the Besòs and Llobregat – to the north-east and south-west, respectively. This was also a time when the overall population of the metropolitan area was still very concentrated in the city, before the more recent, steady out-migration to surrounding towns and counties. Consequently, there was a strong urban aspect to most people's lives. Moreover, the spread of the city was such that large sections of it could be transversed with relative ease. Therefore, it was of a size that could be readily experienced and comprehended, often facilitating and finally resulting in an urban realm of shared associations and meanings among broad segments of the populace. In short, the city had a strong tangibly unitary aspect to its physical structure, that tended, rather naturally, to reinforce attention on its urban-architectural conformation. Indeed, quite apart from remediation of public services, the plans and projects of the late 1970s and 80s, responded strongly and with popular support to this inherent unitary aspect, through piece-meal reconstruction, conservation and mending of the city whole. Barcelona became, once again, the collective possession in a very palpable sense of those responsible for making public decisions and those they served. Moreover, lurking behind their efforts and enthusiasm there also seems to have been a vision of a finished, complete city, or at least one that was very nearly perfectible.

PASSAGES .... *'short in distance but long in time.'*

Carrer Abaixadors

Carrer Carabassa

Passatge Bernadí Martorell

Carrer Aymeric

Peu de la Creu

PLAZAS A PLENTY .... *'to rest and play, dreaming of another day'*

Plaça Reial

Plaça Sant Josep Oriol

Vall d'Hebron

Plaça John Lennon

Plaça del Diamant

Plaça del Sol

Plaça de la Vila de Madrid

Plaça dels Països Catalans

Carrer Hospital and Carrer de la Junta de Comerç

Plaça del Diamant

Plaça dels Àngels

OLYMPIC OPPORTUNITY

Barcelona's successful bid for the 1992 Olympic Games provided yet another opportunity to catapult the city into international attention. It also provided the impetus for a leap in the scale of urban improvements in order to tackle lingering, major infrastructural issues and further redevelopment of key areas, as well as to re-orient the city to prominent topographic features, such as Montjuïc and the coastline, which had been largely ignored or shunned in the past. Planning once again took the form of continued pursuit of projects, albeit often in aggregation and at a larger scale, rather than through the imposition of controls and obligations on prospective property developers. Again, the public sector and most notably the Municipality took the initiative, although with a higher profile of promotional activity and, at the right moments, in joint ventures with the private sector. Investment capital flowed into the city, eventually enabling the Municipality to successfully leverage the Olympic opportunity on behalf of local citizens, although not without strains on local resources. These capital flows were also aided by strength in the Spanish economy, growing at a relatively high rate of five percent per annum, during the mid 1980s, and by Catalonia's ranking at or near the top of national economic productivity over the same period.[1] In shepherding forward this jump in scale of urban regeneration and preparation for the games, the Ajuntament displayed a high level of public commitment, initiative and management efficiency, involving close collaboration of key politicians and public servants, together with well-orchestrated public enthusiasm and pride. As during times in the past, the need to meet timetables, public commitments and international responsibilities softened up the usual political process of development, although this time not as compromises but as inclusive syntheses. Throughout, design and other technical support for urban improvements drew further upon a substantial pool of local talent, now joined by foreign architects and technical specialists. At the end of these efforts, Barcelona became the first city since Tokyo in 1964 to pull off the Olympic 'hat trick,' successfully boosting exposure, image and income, well after the Games had ended.

Lines of Command

The idea, as noted earlier, to celebrate a large international event in Barcelona in 1992 originated in the seventies, when Mayor Porcioles approached a number of outstanding Catalan figures in the city, such as Jordi Pujol and Juan Antonio Samaranch, to cooperate in organizing yet another International Exhibition.

For political and other reasons, however, this suggestion did not materialize, even though there was support from the central government. Then, when Samaranch was competing for the Presidency of the International Olympic Committee (IOC) during the late 70s, he suggested to Narcís Serra the possibility of proposing Barcelona's candidacy as the site for the XXVth Olympic Games in 1992. Shortly after Samaranch's successful election as IOC President in 1980, the mayor contacted him to follow up, officially announcing the city's candidacy in January of 1981. The Olympic bid was then worked on during the remaining year of Serra's municipal leadership and into the period of Mayor Maragall, culminating in selection in October of 1986. Indeed, the final round of elections, at the 91st IOC Session in Lausanne was hardly close, with Barcelona receiving 47 votes to second-place Paris with 23. Furthermore, the games that took place in Barcelona in 1992 were the first since 1972 to be free of boycott and involved some 9,300 athletes from 169 countries.[2] If nothing else, this alone vindicated Samaranch's tireless efforts, over the years, with heads of state and sports leaders from all over the world, to repair the Olympic cause. From early on, Samaranch was a rare blend of sportsman, sporting advocate, industrialist and public figure. He started his political activities in Barcelona's provincial council as the Councilor for Sports in 1954, having been an able athlete, leading the Spanish roller-skating team to a world title. From 1955 to 1966 he was President of the Sports Commission of the Diputació de Barcelona and the Catalan representative on the National Sports Delegation, serving as President of the Spanish Olympic Committee between 1967 and 1970. Prior to his presidency of the IOC, he was the Chief of Protocol in 1968, a member of the Executive Committee in 1970, and Vice President between 1974 and 1978, as well as returning again to the IOC's Executive Board in 1979 again as Chief of Protocol. In between time, Samaranch was also a conventional political figure at both a regional and national level, sometimes in association with Franco's regime. He was appointed Ambassador to Moscow, when Spain restored relations with the U.S.S.R. in 1977. Within the Olympic movement, Samaranch was an entrepreneur, foremost in supporting the commercialization of the Games, primarily through television broadcast rights. He also did more than most, in spite of some early questions about his political past, to restructure and modernize the Olympic institution.[3]

Faced with the challenge of staging a successful sporting event and also accelerating their local agenda for civic improvement, the Ajuntament in Barcelona put together a talented local technical team and a compact though flexible management structure under Mayor Maragall. For some time, Oriol Bohigas had been the most influential figure on matters of planning and urban design in Barcelona, providing intellectual leadership at both a conceptual level – through ideas about emphasizing projects rather than plans and about the potentially positive spreading influence of discrete physical urban interventions, described in chapter two – and in education and mentoring, by guiding Barcelona's younger generation of design talent. This was especially the case when he served as the city's Director of Public Works and, effectively, head of planning, although it continued through later municipal roles, such as the official in charge of culture in Maragall's 1991 council. As noted in chapter two, Bohigas had been a prominent member of Barcelona's architectural scene since the 1950s, with strong ties within the leftist *intelligentsia*. A man of notable cultivation and broad knowledge, he also practiced what he preached, as a senior partner in the architectural firm of Martorell Bohigas and Mackay (MBM), with responsibility for a number of significant Olympic projects. During preparation for the Olympics, Joan Busquets, serving as Coordinator of Planning Services for the Ajuntament, also made invaluable contributions to the overall planning and organization of broad-scale projects and infrastructural systems, as well as negotiating a sense of hierarchy and order of priority for these activities, including inclusion of a role for the private sector. Also coming from an academic background, Busquets taught in the School of Architecture, as noted in chapter two, and was a significant member of the Laboratori d'Urbanisme under Manuel de Solá-Morales, during the early 1970s. There was also a strong contingent of engineers, led by Joan Ramon de Clascà – the City Engineer – and including Alfred Morales, the Transportation and Traffic Co-ordinator for the City Council.[4] Josep M. Serra also served through much of the period as the councilman with oversight on urbanism, public works and municipal services. Finally, there was Josep Acebillo, as noted in chapter two a contributor to Serra's early commission on the urban circumstances of the city and, during this Olympic period, the Technical Director of the Municipal Department for Development and Planning (IMPUSA), having succeeded Bohigas, for the city's 1992 Olympic Games' effort. Acebillo, by now renowned for his hard-driving, uncompromising personality, as well as his broadly-inclusive and synthetic view of urbanism at a variety of scales, is also a local graduate in architecture and was a part-time instructor at the university.

Throughout its Olympic endeavors, Barcelona was largely supported by the friendly, socialist government of Felipe González at the national level. Indeed, apart from anything else, González saw the event as yet another way of celebrating the 500th anniversary of the founding of the 'New World,' in 1992, alongside the World's Fair in Seville. His PSOE – dominated government maintained their majority in the national general elections in 1986 and 1989, although they were run very close by the PP – *Partido Popular* – in 1993, gaining just 159 seats to 141.[5] On the local front it was largely political business as usual, with Maragall's PSC coalition winning the municipal elections in 1987 and 1991, and with Pujol's CiU controlling the Generalitat, over the same period. Although there was a steady decline in the popularity of Maragall's PSC in the run up to the Games, the declination was not substantial, moving from an apogee of 45 percent in May of 1983 to 42.8 percent in May of 1991.[6] There was broad confidence in the socialist party's management of the city and in Pasqual Maragall's personal vision for revitalizing and restoring a "sense of dignity," as he put it, to Barcelona's urban landscape. For him, the relationship between good urban design and social welfare was a strong one. In his words, "sections of the city which are the product of unbalanced speculation, or decay, tell a story of misery, alienation and abandonment. There is a loss of sense. Youngsters shouldn't have to grow up in a landscape which isn't meaningful" – a clear reference to quality design. Further, "you need a minimum critical mass" – referencing again to the quality of the environment and its occupants – "in order to create the spontaneous expansion of wealth necessary for a certain level of vitality."[7] Here, Maragall also seemed to be echoing a similar sentiment to Bohigas' notion of the spread of positive effects from well-gauged urban projects, as well as a staunch belief that it was the role of the municipal government to set and promote standards of urban quality and excellence.

In order to meet the stringent requirements and deadlines the Ajuntament had set for themselves, work on Olympic Games installations and other urban improvements was organized within several public and quasi-public companies – SAs or *Societats Anònimes* – created especially for those purposes, such as Vila Olímpica, SA (VOSA) and the Anella Olímpica de Montjuïc, SA (AOMSA), all grouped under HOLSA – Barcelona Holding Olímpic, SA – the primary holding company responsible for overall management and financing.[8] Technically, the Spanish state had a 51 percent stake in HOLSA, with the remaining 49 percent held by the city. Two subsidiaries of VOSA – the Nova Icària, SA (NISA) and the Port Olímpic de Barcelona, SA (POBASA), also had private capital commitments of 60 and 50 percent, respectively. Essentially, the city and the state endowed the SAs with financial resources in the form of long-term credits, with comfortable prices and repayment terms. HOLSA, in turn, created a depreciation fund permitting the return of the SAs indebtedness over ten years to the principal stakeholders. By no means a new institutional arrangement, for SAs had appeared in Barcelona as early as the 1840s as private stock companies as described in chapter one, they were reintroduced in 1987 by Maragall, as public companies, in order to tackle the large and mounting public work's projects. The essential advantages to the municipality of the SA arrangement were several fold. First, it allowed special technical and managerial teams to be established with expertise and a particular focus on a special kind of public work, without necessarily deflecting from the on-going projects of more generalized city departments. Second, they were a way to bring to bear talent and wherewithal on a temporary basis, for the time necessary to complete the job, without building up a bureaucracy that would eventually become redundant. In fact, HOLSA was abandoned in 1993, shortly after completion of the Games. Third, the controlled, yet arm's-length arrangement from the municipal bureaucracy gave the SA structure both flexibility and efficiency in its operations, as well as certain financial advantages, such as surpassing standard levels of municipal indebtedness. Nevertheless, the SAs still had to comply with local governmental laws and only act on directives from the Ajuntament, which was also legally obliged to control their operations. Revenues were raised through syndication from a variety of public and private sources, with ratings in the market place pegged to the municipality's relatively advantageous rate. Throughout, technical support and guidance was provided by IMPUSA for most, if not all, the SA's design and planning activities.

In many ways the SAs are similar to, say, 'special district' authorities, operating for some time now in the United States and elsewhere. However, they have more of a task force orientation with finite time and financial limits. Sometimes criticized for a lack of transparency in their management and scope of operations, they have proved, at least in Barcelona's case, to be a successful means for pushing major public projects forward in a timely and relatively unwasteful fashion. Their advantage for complex co-ordination among different disciplines and authorities was also amply demonstrated during the Olympic Game's preparations. Although differently organized, the final creation of the ring-road around Barcelona – the Cinturó de Ronda – originally proposed as far back as

1905, was run according to much the same management ethos. Finance and development was shared among three authorities – the Ministry of Transportation and Public Works, the Generalitat de Catalunya and the Ajuntament de Barcelona. However, leadership came through Acebillo and IMPUSA, who together with Alfred Moralles was the essential author of the project. Unlike what often happened elsewhere, when traffic engineering imperatives and requirements dominated the design and construction of a piece of public infrastructure, which could and should have other purposes, engineering and urban design came together in a complementary manner, subordinated to larger ideas about the city. This outcome was particularly evident in the Ronda del Litoral – the seafront sections of the ring road including the Moll de la Fusta, mentioned earlier in chapter two, and the Litoral Avenue of the Olympic Village. There, lanes of traffic were appropriately separated, sunken below grade in some places and well co-ordinated with accommodations for pedestrian activity in order to minimize, as far as possible, any sense of a barrier between the city and the sea.

Despite a determined and well-focused set of managerial arrangements, however, several problems arose. First, the 1985 bid estimate for the cost of the Games preparations of 2.73 billion dollars was exceeded by around 300 percent, costing something like 7 billion at comparable rates of exchange. This cost increase was due to an expanded scope of work and budget overruns on specific projects. The Sant Jordi Sports Palace by Arata Isozaki, for instance, finally cost around 89 million dollars compared to a budget of 30 million, and the Olympic Village came in at around 2 billion dollars, compared to estimates of 1.4 billion dollars. The entire scope of the ring road, including unforeseen elements and, anyway, lying outside of the Olympic budget per se, cost 1.5 billion dollars compared to an earlier estimate of 1.0 billion.[9] Second, the sheer scale and some of the technical sophistication of some of the work taxed local construction capacities. Towards the end, round-the-clock shifts were required. There were threats of stoppages. There was a shortage in specialist trades, and some quality control problems. The technology required for Isozaki's Sports Palace, for instance, was new to Spain and the site on Montjuïc was also difficult to negotiate. Nevertheless, to put the overall effort in some perspective, it was comparable in cost value, again in constant dollar terms, to the continuing 'Big Dig' in Boston – the largest single public works project in the United States – with comparable ambitions to extensively upgrade the city and bring it closer to the sea. Specific budget overruns and capacity problems not withstanding, however, the Olympic effort stimulated around 8 billion dollars in public and private investment for Barcelona, with slightly more than 50 percent coming in public funds, vindicating the city administration's faith in making a leap forward in the metropolitan scale of their urban ambitions and placing Barcelona in a substantially more competitive position among other cities in the European Union, if not in the rest of the world.[10] It also took far less time than Boston's 'Big Dig.' Finally, some resistance had to be overcome to the municipality's plans for public improvements. At one stage, the Generalitat, a partner in the ring-road venture that was controlled by its political rivals, delayed construction and stood against efforts to bring a section of the subway to the Olympic Ring on Montjuïc. There was also controversy among various factions of architects over certain projects, including Santiago Calatrava's communications tower atop of Montjuïc. In the end, however, this political in-fighting and arm-wrestling did not prove to be detrimental to the overall effort and was probably mild, given the width of the political divide between the PSC and CiU. Certainly, it was not lost on those in the Generalitat that Barcelona's success was also Catalonia's.

Olympic and Other Urban Projects

There were four principal sites for the Olympic Games on the edges of the central city and connected by a large ring-road improvement, mentioned earlier in passing – the Cinturó de Ronda.[11] As alluded to, this overlay on the existing physical fabric of Barcelona was clearly beyond the discrete urban interventions of previous years, reorganizing the overall urban form of the city at a perceptibly metropolitan scale. Essentially, the Cinturón de Ronda encircled what was mainly known as Barcelona, with the Olympic Games' sites helping to complete development in under-used zones within this encirclement. In scope, scale and ambition it rivaled the Cerdà plan and construction of the Eixample as a singularly-oriented, physical planning proposal. The four sites were the Olympic Ring on Montjuïc, to the south-west of the old town; the Olympic Village and Port in Poblenou, to the north-east; Vall d'Hebron to the north-west among the hillsides; and an area along the Diagonal, near the university campus, well to the south-west of the city center. Other sites were also used for some of the Olympic sporting events, even reaching as far afield as the towns of Tarragona and La Seu d'Urgell, as well as within Barcelona proper. In addition, the airport and approaches from it to the city were upgraded and improved, and the heavy burden to be placed on Barcelona for telecommunications and other media links during the Games, was taken as an opportunity to provide several striking new installations.

The Olympic Ring – as it was called – played host to major events, such as track and field, swimming, baseball and wrestling, as well as housing the main indoor arena for a variety of sports. Located near the summit of Montjuïc, immediately behind the pavilions of the 1929 International Exhibition, the site already had some sports facilities and was envisaged as the Game's main venue. As early as 1983, the layout of the site was subject to a limited competition, won by Federico Correa and Alfonso Milà, who went on to serve as master planners.[12] Probably initially conceived of as an ensemble of buildings and public spaces around the serpentine Avinguda de l'Estadi, plying between the old exhibition site and the old stadium, Correa and Milà's plan spatially organized the new facilities into a compact, axial arrangement of plazas and buildings, descending down the hillside. In some ways this was a useful approach. It allowed, for instance, for a direct link between the existing stadium and swimming pool facility. It also provided a heightened sense of presence for the overall venue amid the landscape of Montjuïc, which is quite vast. Here, the concept of a main axis – the Olympic Esplanade or Passeig de Minici Natal – was purportedly modeled after the neo-classical arrangement of Lincoln Center in New York, including minor axes serving flanking buildings and plazas, although a similar approach in the EUR for the Rome Games also comes to mind.[13] However, in execution, there does not appear to be quite enough building mass, or specific building elements, to fully hold the conceptual intention together. Oddly, termination of the esplanade in the circular Plaça d'Europa, occurs to the side of National Institute of Physical Education of Catalunya and almost at the same height. At best the composition comes off as a succession of well-made, although abstract plazas and building podia. It also seems like Correa and Milà may not have had sufficient control over the overall plan, given all the actors and intervening interests involved.

The sport's pavilions themselves are an eclectic, although interesting mixture of styles and interpretations. The main stadium – the Montjuïc Municipal Sports Stadium – was originally designed by Pere Domènech and built in 1928, as a part of the International Exhibition. It was neo-classical in overall appearance, typical of many stadia in various parts of the world at the time. Refurbishing and expanding the stadium's capacity for the 1992 Games was placed in the hands of Vittorio Gregotti, working with Correa and Milà. The prominent neo-classical components of the old stadium were preserved and needed additional capacity added by lowering the playing field by some twelve meters and by adding steeply-raked stands on the sides. A large cantilevered, light, metal-trussed canopy was also installed, covering the main grandstand. Gregotti and his colleagues succeeded well in meeting the seating requirements and solved the sight-line conditions for the difficult corner sections of the oval configuration. They also managed to bring an overall sense of architectural coherence and provocative combination of old and new to the complex. Mainly this affect came by way of an apparent refusal to blend or otherwise mix too many building elements together and in the relative scale of the new installations. Certainly, the comparatively intimate theatrical scale of the facility, often rare in stadiums, was on full display during the striking and tasteful opening ceremony to the Games, that in itself, set a precedent that others have followed, as well as for the sporting events themselves.

The most striking installation was provided by Arata Isozaki and Associates, the Japanese architects for the Palau Sant Jordi mentioned earlier – a large 17,000 seat multi-purpose enclosed sports pavilion. At least at the time, it was covered by the largest space-framed dome in Europe, assembled on site and then jacked into place.[14] Restrained, in comparison to some of Isozaki's prior work in the United States and elsewhere, the pavilion was well appointed, although for some, its mosque-like appearance may have seemed somewhat incongruous. For others, especially given the technical bravura involved, it probably recalled Pier Luigi Nervi's Roman Sports Palace of some thirty years earlier. The Bernat Picornell Swimming Pools were originally constructed for the 1970 European Swimming Championships and reconstructed and expanded by Moisés Gallego and Francesc Fernández for the 1992 Games. Already an elegant building in a low-key modern manner, the architects did nothing to upset this impression, refurbishing and complementing the original design in a sympathetic manner. Perhaps most striking was the open frame with V-shaped supports provided to an ancillary building at one end of the pools. The last of the four major installations, in addition to a baseball field, was the National Institute of Physical Education of Catalunya by Ricardo Bofill of 1985 to 1992, that played host, during the Games, to the press corps and for wrestling events. Primarily designated as a teaching facility under the jurisdiction of the Generalitat, one of Bofill's patrons along with the central government in Madrid, the building is neo-classically postmodern in an academic manner, constructed of pre-cast concrete, etched to look like stone. Rather somber in appearance, both inside and out, perhaps playing lip-service to the classicism of the stadium, the pavilion also seems out-of-step with most of the modernistically-inclined architecture being produced elsewhere in the city at the time.

Other installations within the Olympic Ring included the controversial communications tower by Santiago Calatrava from nearby Valencia, a late comer to the venue, and as mentioned earlier, probably required to meet the telecommunication loads of the Games.[15] Rising some 125 meters, the steel tower was twisted and tilted to also act as a sundial. Many in Barcelona's architectural community, as noted earlier, objected to the unusually expressive form, if not to the tower itself. However, its installation and design were strongly supported by local politicians and the Olympic organizing authority. Its setting completes the Monumental axis of the 1929 Exposition, up the slopes of Montjuïc from the Plaça Espanya below. Given both its altitude and the height of Montjuïc, it is also visible from most parts of the city and almost as far west as the airport. Far less immediately visible were the supporting infrastructure and landscape improvements around the Olympic Ring. They were, nevertheless, well-couched within the terrain of Montjuïc and provided a useful level of convenience for spectators coming to the otherwise rugged and somewhat remote site. As discussed earlier, although the hilly outcrop of Montjuïc is relatively close to the center of Barcelona as 'the crow flies,' so to speak, it is a place that has loomed over and been relatively isolated from the city, rather than being fundamentally integrated within its urban fabric. This sense of isolation was reinforced, over the years, as unoccupied parts of the outcrop were used for marginal usage, such as waste disposal, storage of coal, quarrying, and shanty-town squatter settlements. Added to this, the Castell de Montjuïc, still under central government authority, was a symbol of repression and of political incarceration. In fact, Montjuïc remains to be completely developed even for outdoor recreational use. Piece by piece and a section at a time, the city has sought to bring a civic order to the mammoth outcrop, stretching as far back as Forrestier's Jardins Mossèn Cinto Verdaguer on the lower eastern slopes, through the building and garden complex of the 1929 Exposition – both mentioned in chapter one – to the Olympic Ring of 1992. Part of this last phase of re-territorialization on Montjuïc included the Parc del Migdia and Sot del Migdia by Beth Galí of 1989 through 1992, incorporating clear and well-planned approach roads with ample parking, connected to the Cinturó de Ronda behind the main stadium.[16] Within the vast area of the park, extraneous buildings were eliminated, local vegetation was sensibly deployed wherever possible, and an urban character was brought to the roadway and parking system, and an extensive semi-paved outdoor space was provided for major outdoor public events. Perhaps most striking, within this landscape ensemble, were the abstract, minimalist demarcations provided for various activities. Entry to parking areas, for instance, was made between a series of large sculptural, fin-like structures, that clearly acknowledged both the scale of the automobile and of the surrounding expansive landscape. Not able to provide a subway stop on Montjuïc itself, outdoor escalators were installed to facilitate movement, mainly above the lower reaches of the 1929 Exposition site leading to the Olympic Ring from the transit stop in the Plaça Espanya. Finally, few television viewers of the Olympic diving events can probably forget the dramatic pirouetting of the divers above the city stretched out below, from the municipal facility on the side of Montjuïc.

The Vall d'Hebron Olympic area was used to accommodate cycling, tennis, archery, some hockey fields, a pavilion for the Basque game of *pelota*, a press center, some housing, as well as other ancillary facilities. The site is nestled into a hillside below and edged by the Ronda de Dalt, part of the new ring-road improvement, as it passes around the north-western side of the city. By contrast to the axial, neo-classical approach taken by Correa and Milà for the Olympic Ring, Eduard Bru, collaborating with Jaume Arbora and Antoni Balagué, as well as with members of IMPUSA, boldly took on the contemporary problem of a diffuse, heterogeneous and almost suburban landscape in their development planning. For them, a primary problem was how to make public space out of an abundance of open space, quite apart from accommodating a mixed variety of programmatic activities. Moreover, they clearly recognized that other uses – both public and private – might also be attracted to the area over time and, therefore, the idea of finite occupation of the site needed to be open-ended. Instead of creating public and otherwise occupiable urban space through the composition of building elements, they elected to define and give specificity to the site's terrain, in the form of a baseline infrastructure of platforms and edges. This emphasis on topography and topographical manipulation – a common feature of Bru's work – sought to bring both spatial order and opportunity to what was essentially a 'middle landscape' – neither fully urban nor peripheral. Moreover, while this type of approach has gained mounting credibility in recent times, embodied in concepts like 'landscape urbanism,' it was less clear then, during the late 1980s. Essentially, broad platforms were sculptured from the site as a sequence of interlinked tiers down the hillside, each platform more or less accommodating a specific Olympic or other facility. The edges of the platforms were then given rigorous definition – again consistent with the infrastructural analogy – by well-made landscape elements, linear parks, viewing platforms, street furniture, roadways, and paved access areas. In effect, the well-articulated spaces, in and around buildings on the platforms, became a public domain, with almost all components providing an inviting outlook on the city below. Furthermore, an insistence on relatively low-lying horizontal building forms, at least for the institutional buildings and sports pavilions, conformed well to the landscaped platforms, producing further accentuation to an eventual composition of horizontal planes.

Within the master plan and beside the area predominantly set aside for sports pavilions are several housing estates, with rows of apartments rising some fifteen stories above grade, also affording excellent views over the city below. Again, however, the underlying landscape and service infrastructure was shaped to the topography in the form of platforms providing support for either building or community open areas and in a manner that allowed a free-flowing articulation of landscaped space across the site. The high-rise dwellings, for instance, were set on steel frame structures that created an open aperture between the buildings above and the rising grade below, offering both a sense of transparency and formal integration. The primary and secondary systems of community open space also complement the idea of distinguishable parts and places within a well-landscaped whole, dominated by a spacious linear park, leading downhill towards the Club Josep M. Figueres and the Avinguda del Cardenal Vidal i Barraquer, contrived of paved and treed horizontal landscaped areas and broad sloping lawns and pathways. The intermediate zone between the municipal tennis facility and the housing along the Carrer de Pare Mariana leading downhill from the Montbau metro stop, also followed the theme of specific outdoor places within a coherent linear system, although in a more condensed serial manner. In particular, the community open space at the downhill end of the housing, with its paved areas, bosque of trees and cypress groves, offers considerable and useable spatial variety within a relatively small precinct.

Apart from this general horizontal conformance, each of the Olympic facilities had its own character and architectural interest. The Horta Velodrom, constructed on the upper side of the Ronda de Dalt was actually an earlier facility, designed by Esteve Bonell and Francesc Rius and constructed in 1989. The low circular form of its continuous external facade and ring of construction blends well into the undulating topography. Inside, the sloping oval velodrome track is centrally placed at a lower level, providing on open public plaza for spectators in addition to seating, between the geometry of the two main figures of the plan. The Pelota pavilion, sited close to the Ronda de Dalt on the downhill side, known otherwise as the Vall d'Hebron Sports Pavilion, hosts two functions – the Municipal Center for Pelota and the Municipal Sports Hall. Designed by Jordi Garcés and Enric Sòria between 1990 and 1991, externally the pavilion has a restrained box-like appearance, with large skylight pods poking up above the roof line. There is little to no superfluous attention given to the architecture, other than taking up with local exigencies of function, structure and building material. Similarly, Tonet Sunyer's Teixonera Tennis Club is also restrained, as a long, low-lying rectangular structure, hovering above the adjacent tennis courts, systematically organized across the general building platform. The Archery Range, by Enric Miralles and Carme Pinós, by contrast, located on terraces below the sports hall and tennis club, is an essay in wrinkled and crumpled geomorphic forms backed into the terraced slopes, from which the archery ranges fan out. This complex actually incorporates two kinds of facility – one for training and one for competition. The necessary built facilities for the competition range were designed in the form of inclined, pre-cast concrete slabs, some acting as retaining walls while others enclose cavelike interior volumes, lit from the outside by small triangular openings. The practice fields, partially invert this overriding geometry, through a sequence of concrete roof slabs, tilted horizontally, independent of the walls below, with clerestories above. Intentionally or not, Miralles and Pinós' composition appears to be something of a homage to Gaudí, whose Parc Güell is located nearby, with its geomorphic semi-subterranean grottoes and arcades. There is also something of the same sensibility about Esteve Bonell and Francesc Riu's Basketball Stadium, located in Badalona, especially the soaring, angular interior space, with its deep covered metal trusses. Finally, the Olympic installations were not without their accompanying art work, of which Claes Oldenberg's 'Matchbook' at Vall d'Hebron along the Avinguda del Cardenal Vidal i Barraquer, is among the most conspicuous, with its bright primary colors and oversized 'matches' scattered around the intersection, where it stands as a further interpretation or reaction to the rather haphazard prevailing site conditions and tangential thrusts of automobile movement.[17]

Unfortunately, since completion and use during the Games, the predominantly public and institutional areas of the Vall d'Hebron site have become forlorn, dilapidated and covered with graffiti, in sharp contrast to the adjacent residential areas.

In reality this has also been the fate of a number of other public spaces within Barcelona, as already noted earlier, dating back to the urban public space program of the 1980s. Although certainly not unique to Barcelona – indeed, forlorn public open spaces exist in many other cities around the world – several issues do emerge from Vall d'Hebron and other parts of the city. First, it seems clear that too much unprogrammed public space, especially in the absence of demands placed on it during the Olympics, even when well designed, led to extensive marginal areas and blank walls that suffer from abuse. Second, the setting aside of large precincts for sports facilities and associated public uses, although rational in terms of event planning, raises the question of who tends to, surveills and generally looks after these precincts on a day-to-day basis and in the absence of major events. The same seems to hold for large public district parks, like Parc de Clot described in chapter two. Third, regular maintenance is an expensive proposition for a large portfolio of public open space and dilapidation usually results, unless there is a surrogate concomitant sense of ownership by adjacent property owners and communities with enough means to step in and act as effective stewards of the public realm on behalf of others in the city. In short, constant use and public engagement need to be present in order to offset problems of scale, a lack of useful spatial specificity and beleaguered maintenance budgets, in the upkeep of urban public spaces.

The ostensible reason for the Olympic Village – Vila Olímpica – was to construct 2,000 apartments to house some 15,000 athletes and to create an adjoining port facility for sailing competition.[18] Like most other Olympic installations, however, it was also seen, primarily in this case, as an opportunity to rebuild a dilapidated part of the city and to redress a section of the Mediterranean seacoast which was bereft of beaches and polluted. The site in Poblenou, adjacent to the Barceloneta, was formerly an underused railroad yard with some support infrastructure for coastal shipping. It was expropriated and cleared between 1987 and 1989, leaving one rail line running along the coast, mostly below grade. The city's sewer and storm-water runoff systems were also extensively upgraded and expanded around the site in order to eliminate flooding and water pollution. Some five kilometers of beach were recreated, taking advantage of the litoral sand drift, through a sequence of groins jutting out into the sea. Almost half of the site was dedicated to parks, the majority of which were concentrated behind the beach along the coastline. The Ronda del Litoral, part of the circumferential highway improvement, was partially buried behind the beaches, or sunken in trenches crossed by pedestrian bridges, in order to maximize the connection between the city and the sea. Almost for the first time, Barcelona had a well-serviced and viable recreational area on the Mediterranean, close to the center of town. Curiously christened Nova Icària, a name that has really not stuck, city officials were probably trying to recall the moment of republican socialist fervor, discussed in chapter one, when Sant Martí de Provençals was called Icària, before being named Poblenou in 1901, rather than, as one commentator suggested, in direct attribution to the socio-political treatise of Étienne Cabet.[19]

Predictably, given Oriol Bohigas' *suasion* within both the architectural and official community of Barcelona, the master planning for Vila Olímpica, or Nova Icària if preferred, was entrusted to MBM. During a second stage of further refinement at the scale of city blocks, they were joined by Armado and Domènech, Bach and Mora and Bonell and Rius, prior to assignment of specific commissions to architects – most of whom had been past winners of local FAD (Foment de les Arts Decoratives) architectural awards.[20] In fact, some 38 architectural firms participated in the overall project. The aim was to reproduce, in a compressed time frame, the variety and coherence of the traditional city, involving many different actors. Bohigas and at least some of his colleagues, as alluded to in chapters one and two, belonged to a generation who seemed to want to fuse both tradition and contemporary progress at a time during which the Modern Movement was in crisis. This led them in the direction of an urban hybrid between the monopoly of the traditional city and the rationalism of modern dwellings. In this case, they went back to the Cerdà arrangement, with as Bohigas put it "almost-corridor streets and almost-closed blocks," merged with modern residential typologies, either in the form of linear apartment buildings or partial perimeter blocks.[21] Instead of totally accepting the grid structure of the Eixample, however, Bohigas and his fellow planners also superimposed a maxi-grid, more suited to contemporary traffic and building circumstances, by combining smaller blocks, although leaving the now minor streets to pass through, often under segments of building. Although primarily residential, like in traditional urban areas, other uses were also infiltrated into the block scheme, including a sports pavilion by Moisés Gallego and Francesc Fernández, a telephone exchange by Jaume Bach and Gabriel Mora, and a meteorological center by Portuguese architect, Alvaro Siza Vieira. An overriding sense of hierarchy was also incorporated into the plan, centering around the end of the Carrer Marina, with two high-rise 44-storey towers in front of a plaza, containing the monumental Passeig Carles I fountain by José M. Mercé. One tower was an office building – Torre Mapfre – by Iñigo Ortiz Díez and Enrique de León, outwardly expressed by a vertical arrangement of horizontal bands. The other was a hotel – Les Arts Hotel – sheathed in criss-cross structural bracing by Bruce Graham and Skidmore Owings and Merrill, with a commercial complex around its base by Frank O. Gehry and Associates, including the by now famous 'fish,' playfully floating above. This beachfront real-estate was developed as a public-private partnership, with the government retaining about a 40 percent ownership. Within this axial arrangement of towers, the adjacent Olympic port was set off to one side, as a square quay in plan with docking and sailing facilities, including MBM's restrained yet sculptural sailing center. The sense of hierarchy is also reinforced through the Avinguda Icària – the original name, running parallel to the seacoast through the middle of the Olympic Village, terminating to the northeast on the venerable walled enclosure of the Cementiri de l'Est.

As mentioned, the residential blocks combined formal arrangements from modern linear apartment buildings and more traditional perimeter blocks. All are around seven stories in height, sufficient to give an urban scale to adjacent streets and in keeping with earlier building within the Eixample. By contrast to the Eixample, however, most urban block interiors are very open, accommodating landscape in a variety of vegetated and paved formats. Within these parameters a variety of housing emerged. The apartment blocks by Viaplana and Piñón, for instance, offered a reasonably strict re-interpretation of the Cerdà city block, with its chamfered corner and continuous facades. The chamfered corner, however, was also taken as an opportunity to increase the monumentality of the building, through an open enframement of revetments and other facade elements, giving a greater sense of depth and scale to the composition. The apartment complex by Torres and Lapeña, deviates from the original block plan to creatively take up with some of the eccentricities of the site, such as termination of Avinguda del Bogatell – the local diagonal street running through the area. The facades around the almost circular central court were splayed in and out slightly, also incorporating sliding screens across the fenestration, giving a rippling, dynamic affect to the composition. The complex is then crowned with a small tower, elliptical in plan, close to the outside street – the Carrer de Salvador Espriu. The apartment and office building complex by Òscar Tusquets and Carles Díaz, along the same street, is strongly rectilinear and almost classical in form, with a high masonry-columned portico along its length, immediately behind which sit two symmetrically-placed apartment buildings separated to provide entry to the court beyond, on the interior of the site. Running the full width of the urban block, the commercial part of the complex faces Avinguda d'Icària and houses a multi-level shopping mall above underground parking. Changes in level, together with inclined floors, cleverly accommodate the grade change across the site, from the higher level of the Carrer de Salvador Espriu, and without the unduly interrupting the free flowing spatial sequence. An essay in masonry pilasters and deep windows reveals, the architecture of the complex conjures up images of Puig i Cadafalch's much earlier yarn factory of 1909, described in chapter one. Other apartment complexes by MBM, Correa and Milà, Carlos Ferrater, and Bonell, Rius and Gil, among others, only add to the architectural variety of the basic plan's buildout.

The public space of the Olympic Village is also a microcosm of the historic tradition of Barcelona. There are boulevards, *passeigs*, urban gardens, sculptures, and abundance of street furniture and sundry other public urban conditions to be found elsewhere in the city. The coastal park is novel – since none had really existed before – and generally well aligned with differing conditions of urban street edge, meandering *passeig* and the beachfront itself. Striking opportunities were also provided for viewing the coastline and the edge of the city beyond – again novel features for Barcelona. One of the most interesting landscapes within the overall scheme is Poblenou Park and the La Mar Bella sports center at the eastern end of the Village. The center housed Badminton, during the Games, and now hosts Poblenou's district library and archive. Rather than a building 'sitting in a field,' so to speak, a successful effort was made by Xavier Vendrell and Manuel Ruisánchez to blur many of the usual distinctions between built and landscaped structures, lowering the sense of perceptual threshold between one and the other. By contrast, Enric Miralles tortuous steel shelter, along the Avinguda Icària, strongly imposes a third element into the built enclosure and landscape of this public open space. Seen by some to have an almost sinister appearance and by others to appear poetically playful, the large structure of metal shards and twisted forms also resembles the skeleton of some prehistoric species, perhaps beached on the edge of the Mediterranean during earlier times before it advanced seaward.[22]

The intentions of Bohigas and the band of architects were clear. It was to demonstrate how sections of the Eixample could be redeveloped and integrated with the coastline in a manner that respected the historical form of Barcelona and yet updated the city's layout to meet the likely exigencies of the twenty-first century. Moreover, judging by the use of the name Nova Icària for the area in Poblenou, those in the Ajuntament were interested in the idea of a new beginning and for a new Barcelona in microcosm. Certainly those involved deserve credit for moving a long way towards their goal. The maxi-grid arrangement of blocks has proved to be appropriate. The sense of urban hierarchy and street worthiness that was obtained, while perhaps a little fussy at the local level, appears to operate well at the scale of a larger area in the city. One knows where one is and there is little ambiguity about the importance of various parts within the whole. Furthermore, much of the architecture rises appropriately to the occasion, at least from the perspective of individual projects. There are, however, some apparent flaws, even in the overall working method, which time, may well resolve, through other episodes and instances of building. First, the decision to make urban blocks that were partly open and partly closed in their massing, along with the basic choice of building typologies, introduced, perhaps unwittingly, an expressive reading that was neither 'modernist' nor 'traditional.'[23] While this may not be a bad outcome, it also left many interiors of blocks over-exposed and somewhat vacuous. Second, despite attempts to avoid a 'corridor effect' at street level, it did creep in on several occasions, along with a certain monotony in the expressive alignment of buildings to street. The urban design was at its best when a certain eccentricity was allowed, as in at both Bofill's and Torres and Lapeña's complexes. Third, the creation of so much specific articulation tends to dilute the broader built domain of public space. At times it feels overwrought with installations of one kind or another.[24] Fourth, the matter of the towers might also be questioned. At 40 stories or so in height, they are considerably taller than the high rises of the late 1960s discussed in chapter one. To be sure, they have a landmark quality and, from their upper floors, afford extraordinary views of the Mediterranean and the adjacent city. They are also a building type common in many other parts of the world with similar demands for return on real-estate investment. Still, were they absolutely necessary? Certainly, in the past, land marking in Barcelona has been handled in other ways. Furthermore, there is something of a symbolic confusion, where the two towers are unmistakably aligned with the spires of the Sagrada Família straight up the Carrer Marina. Or, perhaps the towers simply update the iconography of Barcelona's urban aspect into the twenty-first century. Finally, the idea of employing many different architects with some latitude for interpretation, in the hopes of simulating, in a compressed time frame, a more 'natural' process of city building, seemed to err on the side of too many differences and unresolved circumstances, as well as not enough background building. Noble though this approach might have been, it probably suffered from insufficient real friction and competing claims among various developmental actors and design participants, that, in the end, could only come from a prolonged period of buildout.[25]

The final major component of the Olympic effort was the Cinturó de Ronda and the one with the largest overall impact on Barcelona. It has already been mentioned that construction of the beltway was, from the beginning, a collaborative exercise between traffic engineers, architects and other associated disciplines, rather than the more usual coping with and embellishing of a traffic artery once it had been constructed or was under construction. Indeed, this collaboration produced many imaginative and, in places, stunning results, through a combination of sensitive road engineering, well-scaled landscape architecture, and accommodation of communal facilities into useable public space. For design, engineering and construction purposes the entire undertaking was divided into sections. For instance, the Ronda de Dalt, around the northern and north-western part of the city, was divided into two sections between the Diagonal to the south and the La Trinitat interchange to the north, which was also treated as a specific entity within the system. The Ronda del Litoral, taking the seashore line, was divided into three sections, roughly between the Zona Franca near the airport to the south-west and Besòs to the north-east. Basically, the aim throughout was twofold. The first aspect was to minimize the barrier effect of a road installation of this magnitude. The second was to provide an appropriate armature around which to actively integrate Barcelona internally, as well as with both the sea and the mountains. It was also to provide for vastly improved circumferential and point-to-point vehicular circulation at a metropolitan scale, something Barcelona had been lacking for a very long time. Generally, these aims were met by providing public venues, within and adjacent to the road rights-of-way for multiple use, usually in the form of service and communal facilities. Also, a repertoire of different roadway crossections was developed and deployed to match local circumstances, often separating lanes of traffic and softening the otherwise massive scale of such a roadway experience. Specifically, as briefly noted earlier these crossections included versions with traffic lanes jutting over others, traffic lanes being covered or partially covered, and traffic lanes being entrenched, often in a step-wise fashion across the broader landscape section. In addition, an attempt was made to thoroughly resolve disparate roadway elements, like flyovers, approach roads, buffer zones, decks with service facilities and large entrance corridors, into a new form of architectural and not simply functional presence.

Among the places where these aims and approaches are both clear and effective, several stand out. For instance, the Nus de la Trinitat – as its name aptly describes – links five main highways into the north-western part of the city. In short, it is a very complex interchange, with flyovers, spiral ramps and sinuous approach roads. Out of what is again often a placeless no-man's land, Enric Batlle and Joan Roig, again working with the IMPUSA team under Acebillo, created a large-scale landscape of considerable visual interest and public amenity. In essence, it is a park that offsets land losses and other effects of the highways on adjacent neighborhoods, incorporating two geometries: one semi-circular, corresponding to one of the basic circulatory shapes of the interchange; and the other oblique and running at angles to the roadway configuration. The curving twin-level promenade, inside the central portion of the interchange provided a strong amphi-theater-like feeling to the composition and its geometry is also mirrored in an extensive water body beneath. Strong bands of tree cover and well-articulated, terraced changes in level made up the other primary elements of this new kind of parkland setting. As noted earlier in conjunction with contemporary interests in 'landscape urbanism,' Nus de la Trinitat park was a forerunner in both conception and execution. Other multiple-use scenarios were also entertained along the length of Les Rondes. The sports facilities located adjacent to the Bon Pastor and Baró de Viver neighborhoods were literally decked over the beltway, offering glimpses from the roadway beneath of the river flowing alongside. The Plaça Alfonso Comín was constructed out of another traffic roundabout and interchange – El Nus de República Argentina – consisting of a soccer field, a leafy public garden, and a traffic control center for the Guàrdia Urbana. In yet another mode, the social center on the Ronda de Dalt by Marcià Codinachs and Mercè Nadal, runs transversally to the entrenched roadway below, linking its two sides and providing accommodations for an old people's home and a center for teenagers. From the point of view of traffic and circulation, Les Rondes proved to be very successful during the post-Olympic period. It had the desired effect, for instance, of relieving throttling congestion in and around the city center, especially along the Diagonal, Gran Via Corts Catalanes and generally through the center of the Eixample. Relief was also provided from mounting traffic volumes along the Avinguda Meridiana, and along the Gran Via de Carles III, in the south-west. Associated traffic management strategies also relieved stop-start congestion, through improved traffic continuity and increases in the possible velocity of traffic flow through many areas.

In addition to the Cinturó de Ronda, two other major city-wide infrastructural improvements made for the Olympic Games were the modification and extension of the airport and the telecommunications tower set on top of the Collserola mountain range, overlooking Barcelona. The air terminal project, by Ricardo Bofill and Taller de Arquitectura, is located outside of the city proper, in El Prat de Llobregat where the primary airport has stood since 1949, including construction of a terminal in 1968 containing a ceramic mural designed by Joan Miró. In Bofill's design, three passenger terminals, including remodeling of the terminal from the 60s, were set out in a line connected at an upper level by an 800 meter esplanade, within which sit free-standing kiosks, shops, display cases and so on, and through which three triangular-shaped boarding bays are connected, with a total of nine boarding ramps to each bay. The architectural expression of the terminal is a curious blend of repetitive classicist elements and high-tech structure, although the dark, double-glazed perimeter sheathing provides a striking external appearance and a certain serenity to lofty internal waiting areas. The Collserola telecommunications tower by Norman Foster and Partners was the subject of a limited competition and intended to unify the organization of numerous smaller communications installations scattered throughout the Collserola hillside. Among the most emblematic structures of the Games, the needle-like form, sheathed half-way up by a finely-wrought metal structure incorporating 13 platforms, the top one of which is a public observatory, the tower is almost an exercise in pure sculpture. Rising some 290 meters above the Tibidabo, the tower is also something of a structural *tour-de-force*, visible from many parts of the city below. Unlike the tower on Montjuïc, Foster's structure gained ready acceptance and also became one of the symbols of contemporary Barcelona.

On display, among the major Olympic installations and other associated improvements, were three historically different physical planning and urban design perspectives. First and as already mentioned, there was the tried and true, neoclassical axial arrangement of built volumes and public space on display at Montjuïc. Second, there was the traditionally-inclined, yet modern arrangement of urban blocks in Poblenou, with parallels to Berlage's Amsterdam South and some influences of Camillo Sitte, quite apart from Cerdà.[26] Third, particularly at Vall d'Hebron and among the landscapes of the Cinturó de Ronda, there was a confrontation with the later-twentieth century urban condition of fragmentation, placelessness, and an inhabited terrain characteristic of many peripheral developments. As discussed, the choices in each instance, were not without merit nor an essential area-specific logic. However, of the three, it was the third that' broke new ground,' as it were, and was the most creatively interesting contribution. Certainly, after 1992 if not a little before, there has been mounting concern professionally, as well as politically, about how to deal with the mishmash, 'junk space,' and fragmentation that has occurred in the wake of much modern urban development in various parts of the world.[27] Elsewhere, one approach has been to fall back into neo-traditionalism, in the hope of bringing to bear some order, but without anything like a full recognition of the post-modern condition many parts of cities now find themselves in. By taking this condition on in contemporary terms, Barcelona's architects and engineers manifested a different approach and one that is gaining in credibility as noted earlier. Indeed, in looking back over the Post-Franco effort of city building to this juncture, many building projects of considerable architectural value were created, but it is Barcelona's public landscape, now in such a variety of forms, that stands out most. It also mirrors the determined vision of those who were guiding Barcelona's urban regeneration, both separately and together within city hall.

Post-Games Hangover

Yet again, as at other times in the past when Barcelona pushed its urban agendas forward strongly, there was a period of apparent inertia following the Olympic Games. Like the proverbial athlete after a hard and successful competition, there appeared to be a moment of exhaustion in the Ajuntament and some casting about for what to tackle next. There was also a loss of enthusiasm among many in the local populace for grand plans and continual urban improvements. Afterall, life was much better now for most than it was before. The city, or so it seemed to many of its citizenry, had achieved the rewards of sufficient notoriety and a certain complacency had set in. Tourism and other related service businesses were on the rise, bringing many visitors and sojourners to the city, attracted by its risen reputation for urban vitality, amenity and chic. Cultural life had also improved correspondingly, especially with the completion of several major venues, put on hold during the frantic latter days of Olympic preparation. The palpable identity of Barcelona, well and truly spiffed up in so many ways, was now at an all time high, placing it more than ever on the rest of the world's 'must see list.' Nevertheless, deeper at home in the city there were other disquietening issues brewing, that for most had little to do with civic refurbishments, in spite of some of the beliefs of their political leaders.

By the time of the Olympic Games in Barcelona, the Spanish economy, along with that of the rest of Europe began to slip into recession, remaining shaky for the remainder of the early to middle-1990s.[28] After the economic buoyancy of the Olympic effort subsided, this state of affairs also settled in over Barcelona. Although inflation remained in check and even declined, economic production across most sectors declined and unemployment rose again, often alarmingly. In fact, something on the order of 100,000 jobs were lost in the metropolitan area between 1992 and 1995.[29] Measured by labor force surveys, which now included many more women, unemployment as a percentage of the total labor force hovered around 20 percent from 1993 on, with youth unemployment at disastrously and unacceptably higher levels. The electorate, at both the municipal and national level, was also having second thoughts about the directions they were heading. In 1995 the PSC dipped below 40 percent of the vote, although Maragall and the socialists maintained control of the Ajuntament with others on the left.[30] At the national level, the government changed hands in 1996, with José María Aznar's right-wing PP coming to power, with 156 seats to the PSOE's 141 seats.[31] González socialist government was clearly under a cloud, ridden by several scandals and with a majority of the electorate feeling that it was time for a change. Given Spain's short democratic political history, no doubt this change was healthy, signaling again, if there was any doubt, that democracy was there to stay.

Another aspect of Barcelona's post-Games let down was due to the preparatory efforts themselves. Relatively speaking, the amount of building construction had been immense and, once completed, there remained substantial excess capacity largely in place. This left construction firms and allied trades scrambling for work, with not enough to go around. Many architects also found themselves without work and the building industry, generally, fell into recession.[32] Certainly other projects were either coming on line or going forward at the time, but at no where near the same scale and sheer level of effort. To make matters worse, general economic conditions, as previously outlined for Spain were also poor, taking the edge off the amount of capital construction that was being ventured forth. Understandably, perhaps, the local authority was also spending less on public works. Some slipstreaming of private investment did occur in the wake of the Games. However, it was also taking time to unfold. Some controversy also arose over the municipal government's activist role in development, including helping private developers and institutional entities organize limited competitions for projects and alleged promotion of specific architects.[33] Far from assuming a 'hands-off' relationship with the private sector on the urban development of the city, the municipality sought to "create alliances," as Maragall put it, among developers and local design talent.[34] Laudable though this kind of intervention might be from the standpoint of seeking to maintain standards and a particular design point of view, a fine line can also be broached when it becomes heavy handed and stifling of other potentially useful opportunities and contributions.

Then too, Barcelona itself no longer had quite the same desperate attraction for outsiders, as it had in the past. Certainly by the 80s, out-migration was occurring and, if anything, accelerating into the 90s. In 1990 the city population stood at 1.6 million inhabitants, now well less than the immediate metropolitan population of 2.3 million people, and the 4.2 million inhabitants of the broader metropolitan region.[35] The larger urban complex of Barcelona was expanding numerically, but also spreading out. With this spread, especially to surrounding counties, came a certain dilution or leveling of the central city's centrifugal influence. It also complicated the politics of urban management and potentially blunted the overall effect of tight municipal controls and project ambitions. Surrounding communities did not have the same urban design standards and commitment to urban architecture as Barcelona. This out-migration was, however, not a bad thing, given the earlier overcrowded condition in many parts of the city, although it also meant that other economic activity followed the population into the periphery and other outlying areas, at least for a time. Indeed, the patterns of economic activity in Catalonia were beginning to change, as now more footloose industries moved away to better locations. The population within the city was also beginning to age, although in large measure this was due to declining birth rates all over Spain. In 1990, compared to twenty years earlier, the proportion of adult population – between the ages of twenty and sixty five – was much the same, whereas the proportion of elderly population had almost doubled and the proportion of younger population shrank from 31 to 22 percent.[36] At least for the time being, the ratio of dependents to those in the labor force remained relatively constant, although the continued competitiveness of Barcelona was becoming increasingly tied to being an effective hub in a broader network of production centers and facilities.

Post-Games Hangover

It was certainly not the case that building came to a halt in Barcelona after the Olympic Games. In fact, a number of significant projects, initiated earlier, came to completion after the Games. As a part of an overall effort to renovate the city, of which the Plaça Glòries Catalanes was a component, the Teatre Nacional de Catalunya by Ricardo Bofill was completed in 1997, having been begun some ten years early, while the adjacent Auditori Municipal Barcelona by Rafael Moneo was completed a year later, having been started in 1988. Both buildings were part of what was envisaged as a civic-institutional complex in the vicinity of the Plaça de les Glòries at the intersection of the Diagonal, the Gran Via and the Avinguda Meridiana. Lacking urban cohesion in the surrounding area, the two buildings, apart from their large volumes and alignments with the Eixample grid, offer contrasting views of similar programs, and, one suspects, of the respective clients in their support for particular architects. Bofill's Teatre Nacional for the regional government, for instance, is overtly post-modern in its historicist expression, encapsulating the building volumes within a columnar temple-like enclosure, with a huge entry portico on the front. Moneo's Auditori for the municipality, by contrast, is configured as a single independent and introverted block, with courtyards inside, the architectural expression of which takes up with the particular modes of its construction with a paneled exterior reminiscent of Louis Kahn's museum on the Yale campus in New Haven, Connecticut.

Another civic complex, within an earlier district renovation plan, key buildings of which were completed after the Games, was located within the dilapidated Raval district on the western side of the Ciutat Vella. The plan was produced by Lluís Clotet and incorporated proposals for consolidation of civic institutional sites and extensive housing rehabilitation. The Museu d'Art Contemporani de Barcelona (MACBA) by the American architect Richard Meier was started in 1988 and completed in 1995, under the ambit of Clotet's overall plan. The nearby Barcelona Center for Contemporary Culture (CCCB) by Albert Viaplana and Helio Piñón, including remodeling of the adjacent Casa de la Caritat, had much the same time frame. With an intricate glazed facade and articulated building volumes, sheathed in white tile work, the museum is clearly part of Meier's personal oeuvre. The building occupies the site of what was once a charitable institution of the neighborhood, along one side of the new Plaça dels Àngels, the surface of which, together with the entrance ramps to the museum, have become a haven for youthful skateboard riders. Viaplana and Piñón brought to bear their finely-wrought minimalist aesthetic on the extension to the Casa de la Caritat around a semi-enclosed courtyard, the huge interior, glazed screen wall of which amply reflects its surroundings while simultaneously dematerializing, as it were, the building volume behind. Other renovations to the Ciutat Vella also included pedestrianization of an extensive network of streets within the denser commercial area. At first keenly resisted by adjacent shopkeepers and merchants, this closure to vehicular traffic quickly proved to be a boon to shopping trade within the area, through the added amenity, safety and comfort that was offered.

Planned renovations to the waterfront of the inner harbor of Barcelona – Port Vell – also reached a stage of completion after the Games, with a strong civic component mixed with private development. The old Moll d'Espanya became the site for a variety of entertainment and related commercial facilities, including the large cubic volume of the IMAX theater by Jordi Garcés and Enric Sòria of 1993 to 1994 and the Aquarium, with its huge 38 meter diameter seawater tank, by Robert Terrades and Esteve Terrades of 1993. The Moll d'Espanya was also linked back towards the city in front of the Mirador de Colom through Viaplana and Piñón's Rambla de Mar and Maremagnum of 1990 to 1995, forming a sinuous, almost floating pedestrian bridge extension of the remarkable Rambla. In common with other cities around the world, the conversion of waterfront use was planned to bring public amenity and new economic value to what had become a picturesque though moribund zone. For Barcelona, it also further reinforced the long sought-after opportunity to bring the vitality of the city closer to the sea. Also, the decision was taken to place the World Trade Center of 1988 to 1998 by the American firm of Pei Cobb Freed on the harbor, making use of the old Moll de Barcelona. The self-contained form of this complex and its large volume, however, looms almost too large within the harbor-side landscape, spatially detracting from the more intricate pattern of neighboring wharfs and buildings with such an abrupt change in scale. No doubt the sheer size of necessary program had much to do with this outcome. Still, the particular formal arrangement only seems to compound the problem. Elsewhere in the city the issue of accommodating large programmatic requirements was handled differently. The L'Illa commercial complex on the Diagonal by Rafael Moneo and Manuel de Solà-Morales of 1986 through 1993, for instance, resolved a large and varied program of uses through an extended block, averaging some eight stories in height, connecting along its entire length, via a single frontage, a number of irregularly-sized building components. Sometimes referred to as a 'horizontal skyscraper,' the 100,000 square meter complex responds to the new exigencies of large-sized commercial development in a manner that produces a well-scaled and generous sense of urbanism, that is appropriate for its prominent site, with an intricate expression of interior semi-public space appropriate for day-to-day activities. Extensive and well-articulated underground parking supports the complex almost across its entire length and a spacious park behind provides welcome open-space amenity for the neighborhood, as well as a vegetated respite for building occupants inside. An otherwise taught arrangement of fenestration across sheer stone-faced facades, was relieved, here and there, to call attention to main entries and through a variegated roofline, reflecting differences in the building volumes and programs behind. A serial, underlying spatial and tectonic logic appears to have been established for the complex, capable of accommodating a variety of local circumstances in a holistic manner.

During the preparatory and post-Olympic period, a considerable amount of remodeling occurred to older structures in the city. Several *fin de siècle* buildings were renovated, including Gaudí's 'La Pedrera,' and others extended and modified in function to capitalize on the growing status of Barcelona for urban tourism. Remodeling of the Picasso Museum and adjacent medieval mansions, for instance, was undertaken in two phases, stretching from 1981 to 2002, by Enric Soria and especially Jordi Garcés, in order to delicately unify and refurbish the ensemble of interior spaces, as well as to better address public ground-floor circulation. Between 1989 and 1992, the old shipyards at the lower end of the Ramblas were renovated by Esteve and Robert Terradas, again with an aim to re-integrate them within the public pedestrian realm of the city. Also at work in these remodeling exercises was careful revelation of the city's historical past together with conscious reframing in a contemporary context. Perhaps nowhere is this intention more apparent than in Ignasi de Solà-Morales' remodeling of the Llimona and Correu Vell Mansions to form the Pati Llimona Civic Center in the old city between 1987 and 1992. Working back to underlying Roman walls, subsequent stages of construction were then also made manifest, culminating in a sheer-walled, contemporary addition, with an elegant metal and glass insert. More completely modern in outlook was the remodeling and extension of the El Corte Inglés, by Torres-Lapeña and MBM, from 1990 to 1994, the large department store built adjacent to the Plaça de Catalunya. A powerful presence, in the response made to the adjacent urban context, the new homogenously stone-clad, large, curved volume of the body of the building, was stretched taughtly around the side, forming a well-scaled background to the spacious Plaça de Catalunya, as well as preserving the landmark quality of Antoni Gallisà's old department store. To either side the building masses and cladding are relaxed to respond in both scale and expression to the continuing urban context along the streets. As such, the overall effect of the project shares contextualizing aspects in common with Moneo and Solà-Morales' L'Illa complex.

In their frenzy to prepare for the Olympic Games and to accelerate their program of urban rehabilitation, almost every conceivable public project was undertaken in a remarkably short period of time by the city. When the construction was finished and the proverbial dust had settled in the post-Olympic period, most of Montjuïc, certainly as it faces the bulk of the city had been transformed, including Carlos Ferrater's topographically-intricate land form for the Botanical Gardens of 1989 to 2001. Extensive areas of the waterfront had been made accessible and returned to the citizens of Barcelona. The Cinturó de Ronda brought needed circulatory access, as well as recreational amenity, to a city that was beginning to choke on its traffic congestion. An airport expansion provided more commodious and presentable connection with the outside world. Numerous public institutional facilities, lacking in prior times, were constructed or refurbished and, needless to say, Barcelona gained an extensive ensemble of sports facilities, rivaling those anywhere in the world. Inroads began to be made into older and dilapidated quarters of the city, particularly within the Ciutat Vella and new ways of building both residentially and commercially within the Eixample, matching contemporary circumstances, was demonstrated for all to see and emulate. Elements of the private sector and organizations within civil society also responded to the leadership offered by the municipality, improving their own facilities and the overall vitality and points of interest within the city. Despite the post-Games let down, the economic downturn, and the shifting in the demographic and related center of gravity away from Barcelona proper, the city had been cannily re-positioned, as a rising urban cultural tourist attraction and service center, with a far broader and complete complement of facilities and accommodations to remain attractive in a changing world. By 2002, for instance, there were nine million night stays in hotels, compared to only three million, prior to 1992. Gone were the days, only some fifteen years earlier, when Barcelona, although always with its own sort of atmosphere, was in such desperate need of so many facilities and amenities of different sorts. The foresight and leadership offered by leaders within the city, at least in contemporary times, was extraordinary, although towards the end, it also raised questions about how far certain agendas could be pushed, before an increasingly well-satisfied and some might say saturated population began to turn in other directions and, further, with significantly raised expectations.

JUST RAMBLING ALONG .... *'side by side'*

La Rambla de les Flors

La Rambla

Rambla de Poblenou

Rambla de Raval

Avinguda Gaudí

Via Júlia

Via Júlia

DOWN BY THE SEA .... *'that's where I'll be.'*

Old Port Towards Montjuïc

Port Towards the Barceloneta

Maremagnum

Rambla de Mar

Parc Litoral Sud

Besòs River

Beaches at Poblenou

Torre Mapfre and Fish

Fish and the Hotel les Arts

BOLD TRANSFORMATIONS

Although much improved, by the late 1990s Barcelona confronted a new round of emerging physical needs, as well as some lingering problems. Fortunately, the post-Olympic hangover had past, economic circumstances had improved, and the capacity for public expenditures had increased. The world outside had also changed. Freer trade and global economic circumstances were increasing competition for goods and services. The so-called 'new economy,' with its emphasis on high technology, communications and knowledge-based industry, was also transforming the way people conducted business and placing new demands on places as desirable locations from which to operate. Closer to home, urban and economic developments in Madrid, as well as in other parts of Spain, now well and truly out of their pre-modern slumber, were vigorously competing for resources and investment opportunities, closing the socio-economic gap with Barcelona and Catalonia. Political circumstances in Spain had also changed, favoring the right and a new private entrepreneurial spirit, and, although Barcelona was beginning to move more fully in the opposite political direction, there was also a heightened sense in the city of the need to court both public and private investment on a broader scale. Indeed, the metropolitan ambitions of those in the city, that began to materialize during the Olympic Games, were being pushed much further forward. Certainly by the end of the century it became clear that Barcelona needed to reposition itself once again in order to continue to flourish as an attractive center for business, commerce and culture. As the sixth most populated regional metropolitan area in Europe, by most counts, the numerical heft to maintain the city-region's prominent position, in most quarters, was already there.[1] However, further attractiveness and prominence would require substantial improvements in infrastructure to combat deficiencies in inter-metropolitan and external linkage. Other issues included: environmental pollution, access to markets and the presence of truly international logistical and convening facilities, as well as perceptions of over-regulation. All would require resolution while still maintaining one of the highest qualities of life in Europe; relatively low skilled-labor costs; and a well-educated, discerning and inventive population. As in the past, substantial parts of what was needed were deemed to be further urban transformations, although this time on a more spatially-dispersed scale.

Pushing Forward Again

During the national elections in 2000, Aznar and his center-right *Partido Popular* (PP) gained a stronger grip on the *Cortes* in Madrid. In fact, after a respectable performance during their first term, the PP gained a whopping 183 seats in parliament against a further decline on the part of the socialists, who slipped from 141 to 125 seats.[2] Earlier, in 1999, Barcelona and Catalonia had moved, relatively speaking and as noted earlier, in the opposite direction. Pujol's party narrowly maintained control of the Generalitat, although being outpolled in Barcelona by Maragall running for the regional government for the first time.[3] This was the first serious challenge by the socialists to the power of the more conservative nationalists in the province, and was a harbinger of things to come and of concerted urban and developmental ambitions beyond the municipality. Joan Clos succeeded Maragall at city hall in 1997 as mayor, going on to lead the socialist PSC to victory in the municipal elections of 1999 with an impressive 44.9 percent of the vote.[4] Clos, a medical doctor with special expertise in public health and epidemiology, began work at the Ajuntament in 1979 as director of the city's Public Health Department. As he recalled, "at that time the thermal inversion and pollution were so bad in Barcelona that you could barely see the Colom."[5] Elected to City Council in 1983, Clos continued his oversight of public health and later, as councilor for the Ciutat Vella, oversaw conversion and upgrading of Barcelona's historical center. No stranger to political leadership, Clos then served as a deputy mayor in 1991 and as Maragall's lieutenant, as first deputy mayor in 1995, as well as President of the Treasury and Infrastructure Commission.[6] Outgoing, energetic and with a quick grasp of issues confronting his city, Clos, like his predecessors, takes a strong interest in the physical realm of Barcelona, alikening his role in this regard as being "responsible for the autography of the city."[7] Judging from efforts under his leadership in the recent past, he also wants to leave his own mark on Barcelona.

Towards the close of the twentieth century, the City of Barcelona found itself more and more hemmed in by the spread of some 30 surrounding municipalities. Its limitation in sheer geographical size, at least in large part, dated back to the Franco era, when the regime adamantly refused to extend any further jurisdiction to the city for obvious political reasons, while simultaneously allowing Madrid to extend its physical limits prodigiously. During the 80s, with an emphasis on retrenchment and redevelopment largely within the scope of Barcelona's 1976 General Metropolitan Plan, size limitation was of little significance. Indeed, for many it was a blessing, by allowing a real focus to be placed on the city's districts and neighborhoods. However, as the metropolitan region began to grow and change and as its standing in the world also rose, the role and interdependent functions of its primary-node of activity – the City of Barcelona – also began to shift, requiring broader support and wider intervention. Ranked at or near the top among larger European cities for its quality of life and employment environment and now as one of the better European cities for business, as mentioned earlier, Barcelona ranked less well with respect to its access to markets, the quality of its telecommunications, external transportation links, freedom from pollution and some aspects of internal transportation.[8] Moreover, the scope and spread of infrastructural improvements necessary to address many of these deficiencies spanned well outside the city as such, into adjoining areas and even further afield, deep into Catalonia and beyond. Specifically, for Barcelona to act as a major transportation hub and regional distribution center, the port and related logistical facilities needed to be vastly extended; the airport needed to be almost doubled in size, especially with rising business traffic and tourism; and rail links, in and out of the metropolitan area, most notably to Madrid and into France, needed to be upgraded and redirected. Further removal of industrial facilities away from the city into more efficient and upgraded locations was also required to help combat pollution and to improve the quality if not the number of employment opportunities, as well as to make room for the rapidly rising service sector. In fact, Barcelona saw a full ten percent swing away from secondary industry, as well as into the tertiary or service sector during the 90s, higher than other parts of the region and than the rest of Spain. The proportion of secondary industry stood at 27 percent in 1991, declining to 17 percent in 1999, while the service sector rose from 66 percent to 76 percent during the same period.[9] Over much the same time, as noted earlier, the population of the City of Barcelona declined appreciably, in relation to the broader metropolitan region, due to out-migration and low natural growth, further diluting the numerical hegemony of the city within the region and its de facto control over centers of population growth. Statistically, over the past 15 years or so, some 250,000 to 300,000 people moved away to suburban and ex-urban locations.[10] In addition, for Barcelona to more fully capitalize on its attractiveness as a destination for international business functions and related activities, larger and better convention facilities were required, as well as improved linkage in these regards with the outside world.

Other issues of a more local nature also confronted the municipality. While there had been a boom in housing construction since the end of the economic recession in 1995, sometimes at high rates of 9 dwelling units per thousand population, housing prices were high, especially in relation to disposable income.[11] Housing mobility also remained low and there was a scarcity factor for many, resulting from unsatisfied demand and a decrease in interest rates and other prices, effectively making housing an attractive refuge from stocks and other earning assets. This was also part of the movement to surrounding and outlying areas, where property was cheaper. In addition, the need to rehabilitate older housing stock also began to become noticeable. Office space, by contrast, remained relatively cheap in European terms, although the absorption rate was not high, actually falling off slightly towards the end of the century. With a GDP per capita close to the average for the then European Union, Barcelona was neither rich nor poor and unemployment, considering black and grey markets, had declined since 1996, although for younger members of the potential labor force it was still relatively high.[12] Diversification, especially among medium and small manufacturing companies, accounted for around 25 percent of Spanish exports, although this had been higher in the more distant past, before the current push towards the service sector. Still, some 260 companies provided jobs for 500 employees or more, a relatively stable record, even if most large companies were now located in Madrid because of its position as the national capital and because of substantial recent privatization of state-owned monopolies headquartered in that city. In fact, labor productivity, while still high by national standards was well below Madrid's, over the period from 1995 to 2000.[13] Levels of public sector investment also showed disparities between Catalonia and Spain as a whole, at about one third less, even with comparable levels of municipal investment. In absolute terms the amount of public investment had risen, since the lows of 1997, although at century's end they had not reached the levels of ten years earlier.[14] In sum, while Barcelona was certainly not broke in any appreciable sense, concern had started mounting over its competitiveness and ability to go it alone, without a substantially more regional metropolitan effort and set of strategic initiatives.

Then too, economic circumstances in the outside world had also changed, as noted earlier. The so-called 'new economy,' which arrived in the early 90s only to stall later on, continues to place new demands on knowledge-based and communications' industries, turning the world, at least in part, into what some have called an 'information society.'[15] In general, Barcelonians have been slow to react for a number of speculative reasons, despite the city's prominence in print and other related media, making it the Spanish publishing capital of the world. First, as one commentator put it, Barcelona is not inherently a "success culture," placing a premium on "engineers rather than on entrepreneurs" – perhaps the *seny* factor again.[16] Second, there is an apparent reluctance to more freely share ideas, a necessary ingredient in market places propelled by venture capital. Third, there is a certain traditionalism associated with enterprises in Barcelona, like with the shop keepers and merchants of old, and proclivities towards family-held companies and not towards broader and more open corporations. Fourth, while public tertiary education is good in many quarters, concentrated and high investment in research and development for information technology has not been a conspicuous part of Barcelona's academic and related commercial panorama, certainly in comparison with other places in the world. In short, it is not entirely the case that Barcelonians were caught napping by the onslaught of information technology, although this was probably partly true, but rather that an abundance of deeper and longer-term cultural ingredients were somehow missing. Indeed, if one surveys the silicon 'valleys' and 'alleys' in the contemporary world, one usually finds a significant amount of government-sponsored support and relatively long-term developmental and entrepreneurial gestation periods involved.[17] Advances and applications in information technology are not something that can be simply turned on by a proverbial switch.

The story about the rise of 'Silicon Valley' in northern California is well known.[18] Its rise and current prowess in information technology was due to regional advantages and what might be called historical accidents. Moreover, as alluded to above, it did not happen overnight. Located in an area, roughly 48 kilometers long by 16 kilometers wide, stretching between San Francisco in the north and San Jose towards the south, the economy of Silicon Valley is dominated by theoretical and practical technological research around Palo Alto in the north-west, closely associated with Stanford University and the Stanford University Research Park, and by semi-conductor firms in places like Sunnyvale, Cupertino and Mountain View further to the southeast. The southern part of the valley, by contrast, is relatively poor. The regional advantages enjoyed by Silicon Valley have and continue to be proximity to world-class academic institutions, particularly at Stanford University and the University of California at Berkeley, with strength in information technology and related fields of research. Also of importance are the collection of highly-talented scientists and other researchers attracted to the place, not least by its pleasant climate and social atmosphere, and also by its preferred location for military procurement of semi-conductors and other products.

The history of the rise of Silicon Valley as a center for high technology began as far back as the 1920s when Stanford University decided to improve its prestige by actively hiring respected faculty, mainly from the East Coast. One was Fred Terman from MIT, the Dean of Engineering at Stanford during the post-World War II years, who was not only a cutting-edge researcher and true intellect in the field, but also encouraged his students to market new technology as it became developed.[19] For instance, he strongly supported efforts by David Hewlett and William Packard to commercialize the audio-oscillator, a key component in the embryonic digital field in the late 1930s. By 1950, twelve years after its founding, Hewlett Packard had some 200 employees and sold around 70 different products.[20] Perhaps more significantly, they also pioneered the so-called 'Silicon Valley management style' by treating members as part of a larger family. In 1954, they accepted Stanford University's offer to rent part of the new Stanford Research Park for their operations, laying the foundation for an unprecedented agglomeration of high-technology industry in Palo Alto. At much the same time, during the 1950s, the semi-conductor industry was born in Silicon Valley with, for example, William Shockley's development of the transistor. Over time this led to formation of the Fairchild Semiconductor Corporation, which, in turn, spurred some 70 companies as either direct or indirect descendants. Government support was also forthcoming in increasingly large amounts, beginning through the relocation of Lockheed – a major military contractor – to California in 1956. From its inception, those working in technology within Silicon Valley developed their own unique culture. First, they saw themselves as modern-day pioneers and were especially responsive to risky ventures. Second, there was and continues to be a high level of camaraderie, leading to broad networks for idea sharing and technical assistance among different firms. In fact, the motto among many became 'competition demands continuous innovation,' which, in turn requires cooperation among firms, who otherwise compete fiercely with one another.[21] As a consequence, occupational mobility has remained high, aided by numerous potential employers and no need to change house, lifestyle, or school district. Indeed, if anything, among the numerous knowledge workers in Silicon Valley, there is a strong allegiance to technology and a habit of following scientists and engineers, rather than firms. There is also the common practice of 'comparing notes,' so to speak, through numerous and varied social contacts.[22]

Industrial development around the Boston metropolitan area's Route 128 was another early mainstay of high-tech information-oriented business in the United States. Intense development also began in the years following World War II and was fueled by proximity to world-class universities in science and technology, such as Massachusetts Institute of Technology (MIT); heavy federal-government spending; and the entrepreneurial efforts of luminaries in the field of information technology, such as An Wang.[23] Geographically, Route 128 is a highway surrounding the inner municipalities of the Boston metropolitan area, some 104 kilometers in length, that formed part of the interstate highway system, also developed during the postwar era. With good access to markets and to prospective employees in Boston's suburbs, as well as to ample land available for development, the zone around Route 128 and especially around radial routes leading out of the city, proved to be attractive to new industrial parks, shopping centers and ancillary office complexes. Particularly during the 1970s and 80s, what would become distinguished high-tech firms, such as Raytheon, EG and G, and the Digital Equipment Corporation, moved into the area. As these and other companies, like Lotus Development, grew in size, they also attracted other smaller service companies. In 1990, there were about 3,000 high-tech firms in Massachusetts, principally concentrated around Route 128.[24] Unlike Silicon Valley, however, the interaction among companies was far more hierarchical, largely according to scale, and occupational mobility among employees was much lower. Also unlike Silicon Valley, there was more of an emphasis on convention, decorum, self-reliance and traditional notions of loyalty to firms. In short, there was a different corporate and related social culture in play. Among the top five states in the U.S. in terms of receipt of federal research resources, there was also a strong federal-agency presence, through the Department of Defense, NASA, the Department of Energy and the National Science Foundation. In fact, during the 1990s the federal government spent something like 60 percent of its defense spending on research in the state and often around Route 128.[25] MIT, in particular, like Stanford, has also been a source of almost endless world-class scientific and engineering research, with alumni and many others associated with the university becoming involved in private research and development.

Bangalore, the capital of the state of Karnataka in southern India, although perhaps less advanced than either Silicon Valley or Route 128 in high-tech development is, nonetheless, significant and shares commonalities with its American counterparts. It is well-urbanized, but again with considerable environmental amenity as India's 'garden city.' In fact, it is the fifth largest city in India and one of Asia's fastest growing metropolitan areas.[26] With good access to the outside world by rail, road and air, the city is also well connected into a broad transactional network, not the least of which is via Internet and a growing industry in out-sourced services from more expensive centers of labor in the U.S. and other parts of the developed world. Also like its American counterparts, Bangalore has a relatively long history of involvement with science and technology, dating back at least to 1947 when the Indian government decided to focus on the development of indigenous efforts in these areas. In 1973, the now prestigious Indian Institute of Management Bangalore was founded, with strong deliberate ties to the fledgling high-tech industries.[27] Located on a 40 hectare site in sylvan surroundings, the campus has been and continues to be the cradle and managerial 'think-tank' for many of India's new industrial entrepreneurs and businesses. Looking for stable and well-supported centers in which to locate branches of their businesses, foreign firms have also invested significantly in Bangalore. For instance, General Electric located its John F. Welch Technical Center there in 2000.[28] Overall, again partly like Silicon Valley and Route 128, Bangalore's technological contributions are mainly in information technology, aerospace and bio-technology. More recently, other areas in southern India are also competing with Bangalore, such as Hyderabad, especially as off-shore outsourcing market places. In large measure, this expansion is due to the entrepreneurial culture of many parts of southern India and its relative freedom from the socio-political tensions and conflicts of the poorer north.

Despite strong government backing, there are also less successful models of industrial development around information technology. Malaysia's Multimedia Super Corridor, for instance, was the subject of a bold government plan in the mid 1990s to push the country into the information age. However, it became the victim of heavy official oversight – the opposite of, for instance, Silicon Valley – and slack investor interest, particularly from outside.[29] Matters were also not helped by the South-East Asian economic crisis, during the late 90s, and the Malaysian Prime Minister's apparent anti-Western attitudes. More significant, however, has been the sheer shortage of indigenous knowledge workers and a lack of financial support for local firms and 'start-up' companies. China's Zhongguancun high-tech zone in north-western Beijing has also not faired well, despite strong government backing, dating back to the 1980s in the form of tax incentives and other business perquisites. Located close by both Beijing and Tsinghua universities, perhaps the two pre-eminent centers of learning in China, many firms are spin-offs from university research and development. However, they have generated little by way of innovation, adapting and trading, instead, on foreign technology.[30] They are also highly dependent upon domestic capital, often not in abundance, and the location in the Haidan district chronically suffers from poor infrastructure. Interestingly, a more viable alternative location to Zhongguancun has sprung up in Chaoyang on the fashionable eastern side of Beijing. This is also Beijing's most international quarter, with high-quality infrastructure, direct access to the airport, and numerous luxury hotels and grade-A office space. So far, Chaoyang has been attractive to well-known foreign firms, like Hewlett Packard, IBM and Cisco, as well as the site of many smaller image-conscious 'start-up' Internet firms. Singapore and Hong Kong continue to vie with each other, although now also over information technology, and once again the contrasting styles of urban management between the two cities are evident. Singapore, has recently become active, primarily through its Infocomm Development Authority, in the information technology market place, by investing in particular industries and shepherding choices from the 'top,' among various potential forms of technical development.[31] For its part, Hong Kong has adopted a laissez-faire approach, again typical of that city, through information technology and policy boards that remain relatively detached from day-to-day business. There has also been a very recent effort to concentrate research and development activities, largely through private funds, in a place called Cyberport, relatively close to Hong Kong University on Hong Kong Island. At this stage, Singapore may be risking too much governmental direction over its information technology activities, whereas Hong Kong may be leaning too much towards the market place. Both places also do not have long histories or profound depth in related indigenous research and development activities.

Among international developments in information technology, the model perhaps closest to Barcelona's cultural profile is Silicon Alley in New York. Located in lower Manhattan roughly stretching in a five kilometer strip from Chelsea on the west side to the tip of lower Manhattan and running through places like SoHo, Silicon Alley has a strong artistic and media-related orientation to its products. By 2001, some 700 hardware and software firms were located in the area, although with a work force with a radically different profile from, say, Silicon Valley or Route 128, with artist and writers representing 48 percent and programmers and engineers less than 25 percent.[32] As a consequence, some believe that Silicon Alley will not remain close enough to the processes of hard-core innovation necessary to become a true center of cutting-edge technical activity. Rent in the area has also proven to be high, perhaps too high, and a number of earlier major firms have now disbanded. Unlike both California and Massachusetts, there also appears to be less access for fledgling firms to venture capital, with would-be investors traditionally vested in retailing, manufacturing and franchising. In fact, in this regard New York ranked behind California, Massachusetts, Texas – with Austin being another prominent center of information technology – and Tennessee in the magnitude of investment in information technology.[33] In short, information technology can be a fickle business, in spite of proximity to first-rate research institutes, a well-trained labor pool and considerable urban amenity. The most successful centers also have a history of being in the business, are at the leading edge of technical innovation, have well-established although different working cultures, a blend of other kinds of high-tech development, and considerable sources of long-term financial support. They also have achieved a critical mass, the necessary scale of which is quite high.

Finally, transportation mobility, internal to Barcelona, has received low ratings in the past, detracting from the city's attractiveness for business. However, it has been improved substantially. As discussed in chapter three, the impact of the Cinturó de

Ronda including its access roads has been substantial in relieving traffic congestion in and around the central city, as has improved traffic management. Modal shift in favor of public transportation has also shown signs of improving and there has been a continual evolution of the metro subway system – run by the Transports Metròpolitans de Barcelona (TMB) – over the past twenty years or so. Between 1980 and 2000 extensions were made to lines 1, 3, 4 and 5 within the system and a new line – line 2 – was added.[34] Largely, the metro runs as a radial scheme emanating from the center of the city, particularly from the Plaça de Catalunya, but with some closer-in circumferential movement made possible by changing from one line to others. Circumferential service further out in the network towards the periphery of the city, unlike, say, in Tokyo, remains awkward, requiring trips in towards the center of town and then out again. Still, only 19 percent of the geographic area of the municipality is not served by the metro and some extensions have been made to neighboring communities, like Llobregat, Besòs and Badalona.[35] With regard to environmental pollution, another negative factor in the attractiveness of the city, substantial improvements have also been made. Atmospheric emissions were curtailed through the closure of many city industries, although over the ten year period from 1987-1997 air pollution, on the whole, increased by around 23 percent and remains above the Heidelburg objectives set for 2005.[36] Sources of water pollution have also gone through a similar clean up through industrial relocation away from the coast, although both the Llobregat and Besòs Rivers are still below standard.

River to River Transformations

The so-called 'River to River Transformations' of Barcelona and its immediate metropolitan area are in various stages of planning and completion. While each project has its own identity, specific objectives and institutional arrangements, the broad underlying logic is to sustain and advance Barcelona's economic competitiveness, especially with regard to needed improvements in infrastructural, logistical and other facilities, outlined earlier.[37] Old agendas concerned with upgrading the sea front, neighborhood and district-wide improvement, as well as provision of environmental amenity, are also evident. Stretching from the Besòs to Llobregat Rivers and beyond, schematically the improvements can be geographically subdivided into those in the northern and north-eastern part of the city and those in the south and south-west. Furthest along towards completion are the transformations within a 'triangle' moving back from the seacoast – roughly bordered by and including the Sagrera high-speed rail station and related improvements around Sant Andreu;

the cultural zone around the Glòries Catalanes; area-wide improvements within Poblenou under the rubric 22@BCN; and the site at the end of the Diagonal, ostensibly for the staging of Barcelona's Fòrum 2004, another in the line of international events aimed to draw attention and attract financing for public improvements to the city. In the south-west, transformations include: landscaping of the top hills of Montjüic; various urban improvements along the Gran Via Corts Catalanes, such as expansion of the Fira 2000 trade fair facilities; and the so-called 'Delta Plan' and fuller expansion of the airport in El Prat, together with further rationalization and expansion of the port and related logistical facilities.[38] Most of these transformations are clearly aimed to build on Barcelona's earlier successes in areas like trade, commerce and cultural tourism, as well as to position the city and its surrounding area as the primary destination, mode of activity and distribution center for a much broader region within the Spanish and, consistent with past ambitions, European and international contexts.

After a considerable amount of wrangling over routes, tunnel alignments and station stops, the Municipality of Barcelona, the Generalitat and the Spanish Ministry of Public Works agreed on a plan to construct the AVE high-speed train service, linking Barcelona with Madrid and also, in the other direction, to France. The main inter-modal and service center will be located in and around the existing Sagrera Station, with further stops at the main central station at Sants and at the airport. When completed, the AVE facility will significantly broaden Barcelona's catchment area and also boost its position as southern Europe's high-speed distribution center. For instance, someone in Montpellier, France, would have the choice of taking an intercontinental flight from either Barcelona or from Paris. Travel within Spain will also be greatly facilitated, especially between Barcelona and Madrid, as well as among other major cities within the eventual AVE network. Construction of the station and the servicing yards will make use of the existing railroad rights-of-way in Sagrera, currently held by RENFE, together with GIF the state-owned railway company. The station itself will accommodate metro, bus and regional train links, as well as the AVE, and extensive parking, all facilitating inter-modal transportation transfers. Overall, the total facility will be designed to accommodate on the order of 39 million travelers per year. Above the station, which will be primarily underground on several different levels, a new center will be created, bringing with it new urban activities, development potential and improvement to the zone between Sant Martí and Sant Andreu, historically a working class area of the city now co-mingled with underused or abandoned industrial sites. Some 180,000 square meters of facilities are to be built immediately above and adjacent to the station, including a hotel and offices. In addition, 7,500 dwelling units of social housing are planned to be provided, together with sites for mixed-income, market-rate units.[39] As far as the timetable for the high-speed rail is concerned, the link to Madrid is scheduled to be completed by 2010, with the connection to Marseille coming on line around 2015. Certainly for Madrid, if not Barcelona, the network will be a boon, eventually planned to bring all Spanish regional centers to within three hours or less of travel time from the national capital.

In essence, the plan around the Sagrera station seeks to reconcile and redistribute land uses and buildings across what is now a relatively open seam within the city, made up of railroad tracks, platforms and sidings. The new center will have a strong urban character, in keeping with adjacent urban areas, with a plaza next to the station entrance and concentrations of office facilities. Railroad tracks entering the station are also to be covered in a manner which will accommodate a 3.5 kilometer length of linear park, encompassing an area of some 300,000 square meters and bringing needed public open space to this north-western portion of Barcelona. A Mobility Museum and office complex, by Frank Gehry, is being designed on a site about halfway along the length of the public park, rising to a height of about 170 meters, with the exhibition space appearing to sweep up towards the offices from the base of the complex.[40] Major thoroughfares crossing the station and linear park development are to be respected and integrated within the overall scheme, as well as the La Maquinista housing and shopping center developments, recently completed on the eastern side of the tracks at the northern end of the proposed linear park. There is a good rationale for a Mobility Museum and its location in this part of town. In the past, Barcelona had been at the forefront of transportation engineering and the area around the site was where rail rolling stock was produced, along with more esoteric forms of transportation like the Pegaso sports car and now parts for Daimler Benz. The La Maquinista shopping center by the firm L35 or Galan and Mendoza; the adjacent park; and housing development, planned and partially designed by Joan Busquets, offer a skillful, modern interpretation of how to deal with difficult, irregular site circumstances and create a strong urban texture within largely still open areas of the city. At a floor-area ratio of between 1.2 and 1.3, the housing area is relatively dense, though low rise, including a project within the overall plan by Josep Lluís Mateo with strong horizontal lines. These projects also provide a useful termination to the extension of the Rambla de Prim from the sea coast and an entrance to Sant Andreu, on the other side of the existing RENFE rail facilities.

Again, in keeping with recent public practices, financial and related implementation of the Sagrera project is to be entrusted to a *societat anònima* called Barcelona Sagrera Alta Velocitat, SA, made up of the three principal stakeholders: the central government in Madrid, including RENFE and GIF (50 percent); the Generalitat (25 percent) and the Ajuntament de Barcelona (25 percent). Within this arrangement, the Secretary of State in Madrid will serve as the president of Barcelona Sagrera, SA, while the mayor of Barcelona and a representative from the Generalitat will both serve as vice presidents.[41] In effect, this equal apportionment between the central government in Madrid and the local constituencies means that either no one or any administration has a majority, although the municipality has been designated to take primary responsibility for the design process, ably led at the time of agreement by Josep Acebillo, who was serving a term as both Chief Architect of Barcelona and Commissioner for Infrastructure and Urbanism under Mayor Clos. More important for Sagrera, he was and remains the chief executive officer of Barcelona Regional, charged under contract with technical formation and review of the project. No stranger to public office, having played a fundamental role in the Olympic projects as described earlier, Acebillo, with this dual role, had the responsibility of an unusual concentration of planning and urban design power and authority. Indeed, this responsibility extended to oversight and creative direction of almost all the projects in Barcelona's 'River to River Transformations.' In 2002, the estimated cost of the Sagrera urban development was placed at around 1.4 trillion euros.[42] Although to be strongly led by the public sector, for afterall this is largely a public transportation facility, private sector participation will be necessary to round out all the planned development. Essentially, the developmental model, by now familiar for Barcelona, is to involve a public company as a special authority, charged with orchestration and completion of the work, representing government stakeholders and working alongside of and in concert with private companies and their investors. Originally scheduled for initial service from Madrid to Barcelona to co-incide with the Universal Forum of Cultures in 2004, probably unrealistic at the time of the initial agreement to undertake the project, the infrastructural improvements are now beginning to get underway.

Further completion of the cultural zone around the Glòries Catalanes, a second project area within the northern and eastern 'triangle,' also now well underway, involves an assortment of cultural facilities, along with offices for public authorities and municipal administrators, together with re-reconstruction of the Glòries itself. Probably the most controversial addition to the area is the Torre Agbar of 1999 to 2005 by Atelier Jean Nouvel, the new home of Aïgües de Barcelona

– the water company. Rising 142 meters above grade, the cylindrical free-standing tower with a domed top is shrouded in a continuous surface of small, glazed and multi-faceted panels, that both reflect and refract light in unusual ways. The building encompasses about 51,000 square meters of floor space, making it very large by Barcelona's standards, accommodating offices, services, and an auditorium. The geometry of each floor plate is oval, rather than circular in shape, and within the top portion of the building the floor plates are separated from the external skin of the building, forming a multi-storied structure within the overall tower. According to Nouvel, water as a substance was part of the inspiration for the project, speaking of its vibrant, transparent, luminous and spectral properties.[43] The tall monolithic form can be seen from many parts of the city and raises again the question of the desirability of towers in Barcelona, an otherwise dense, horizontal city in overall aspect. As one of the major intersections in Barcelona, the Glòries Catalanes is certainly spacious enough and potentially monumental enough to entertain such a building. It is, however, the reciprocal reading of public space that's potentially called into question here and in a manner that breaks substantially with existing local precedents. Some admire the building as being distinctive of a contemporary spirit in Barcelona, while others are less kind in the allusions the tower seems to conger up.

Another three building complexes, which will complete building around and within the Glòries, were the subject of competitions, now a familiar part of Barcelona's architectural landscape, held in 2001. The 'Torre Laminar,' by Federico Soriano from Madrid will be located across from the Torre Agbar on the city block defined by the Gran Via Corts Catalanes, the Avinguda Diagonal, the Carrer Ciutat de Granada with the Glòries itself, forming with the Torre Agbar a perceptual gateway to the 'lower Diagonal,' which, incidentally, was not fully completed as a thoroughfare until the 1990s. Rising some 20 stories in height, the 'Torre Laminar,' as its knick-name suggests, will be a broad slab-like building, with an irregular though generally curvilinear floor plan, sheathed in a complex, high-tech curtain-wall system, which again aims to interplay actively with light and prevailing solar conditions. Officially called the Edifici Administratiu Diagonal-Glòries, this free standing edifice will house administrative offices, as part of a move to decentralize the presence of the municipality within the city, together with auditoria and other public spaces at or near the ground floor. Although expansive in both its horizontal and vertical dimensions – somewhat like a giant 'shower curtain' – the building proposal does acknowledge both the sheer scale and directionality of the spatial urban condition presented by the Glòries. In the opposite direction across the circular intersection adjacent to the Auditori de Barcelona, will be the Plaça de les Arts, by Zaha Hadid – a complex of performance spaces for cinema, video and a variety of related events and festivals. Bounded by Bolívia, Tànger and the Avinguda Meridiana, the site for the complex presented difficulties in reconciling grade changes, roadway and railway alignments. Rather than another building per se, Hadid's proposal is more a plastic topography of constructed spaces to accommodate functions; sweeping infrastructural elements to facilitate pedestrian movement across the site and to sites beyond the Meridiana; and ample well-scaled open space, capable of accommodating a variety of activities. Despite the unconventional curvilinear format, the complex is underpinned by a rigorous array of structural elements well fitted to functional requirements, including parking and parsimonious reconciliation of the difficult inherent pre-conditions of the site. Finally, the third building complex, by Martorell Bohigas and Mackay (MBM) is to be the Museu del Disseny de Barcelona – a collection of exhibition spaces dealing with industrial design, ceramics and other aspects of the decorate arts that, up to now, remain scattered less effectively throughout the city. MBM's proposal, which overlaps with the circular roadway system of the Glòries, is straight-forwardly rectilinear in plan, while using the cross-section through the main structure to provide for a variety of exhibit and ancillary spaces of a variety of sizes. It will also accommodate pedestrian circulation across a significant grade change through the Glòries and provide appropriate mediation with an existing local residential neighborhood on the edge of the Glòries, including a park with a large water body within it. In effect, not out of keeping with its site circumstances, the museum complex expressively and functionally engages with the traffic movement – vehicular and pedestrian – both within and through the Glòries. Further renovations to the area are likely to see removal of the market on the north-west side of the Glòries – for some a controversial issue – and creation of more opportunities for housing. Overall master planning undertaken largely by municipal staff, under the direction of Acebillo and Joaquim Español, has been largely contingent on specific project proposals, rather than on some broad formal overriding idea for the area. In fact, as of this writing, several different concepts for how to deal with the overall landscape of the Glòries were still being pursued.

Area-wide improvement of Poblenou – the third component of developments within the 'triangle' – is slated to transform around 1.2 million square meters of old, under-used or abandoned industrial property into productive use.[44] As described in chapter one, Poblenou arose as a factory and poor, working-class area on the outskirts of the city during the industrial boom of the nineteenth and earlier twentieth centuries. Indeed, conditions were so bad at the time that it became known as a place "where people were born old."[45] Moreover, as the years past,

Poblenou remained primarily an industrial precinct, with factories and related warehousing activities co-mingled with housing and local commercial uses within the nominal extension of the Eixample, primarily on the seaward side of the yet to be completed Diagonal. A major round of improvements came to the area in the guise of the Vila Olímpica, as described in chapter three. However, extensive areas of the district remained relatively untouched, even after industries and other enterprises had migrated elsewhere in the metropolitan area in search of larger and more efficient sites. Strategically, within the city the municipal government now see the area, perhaps over optimistically, in a manner analogous to New York's Silicon Alley and are proposing infusion of 'new economic' activity in the form of knowledge-based industries built around information technology and media, along with similar conversion of industrial buildings into loft space for both living and commerce. The proposed plan for the district, which inscribes a patchwork of broad areas, provides, in aggregate, for the potential of 3.5 million square meters of housing, including around 4,000 new dwelling units under statutory protection, averaging around 85 square meters of livable space per unit; together with 3.2 million square meters of new economic activity; 75,000 square meters of green open space; and 145,000 square meters of public facilities in support of local circumstances. In addition, plans are afoot to establish a strong university presence in the area, principally under the auspices of Barcelona's fourth public university – Universitat Pompeu Fabra and its new audio-visual campus. Projections cite anywhere between the creation of 110,000 to 130,000 new jobs in the area, along with a wholesale, block by block re-conversion of many parts of the district.[46]

Once again the municipality is taking the leadership and a strong hand in the urban transformation. Predictably a *societat anònima* has been established to oversee and guide physical improvements, called 22@BCN, SA in keeping with the new technological flavor they hope to bring to the district and because of the rezoning within 'type 22' of prevailing use regulations required for the major urban blocks up for renewal. Also, once again specific projects are to be let within an overall plan.[47] However, this time the plan also defines potential building blocks more in terms of rules and guidelines to be followed rather than as static, masterplan prescriptions. Indeed, one early exercise during the overall process, that occurred around 2001, was to simulate various outcomes for the overall planning rule structure and to demonstrate, through design, both the necessity and feasibility of various concepts about easements, parcel sizes, amounts of open space, heights of buildings, allowable dimensions of floor plates, setbacks, and so on. Given the need for the private sector to accomplish most of the building and many of the infrastructural improvements, this newer tactic was warranted and closely matched similar prescriptions in places like the U.S., where regulatory control and urban design guidelines are heavily relied upon to produce desirable results. So far, generally the response to site constraints on the part of the private sector has been positive, particularly with regard to adequate provision for both small and larger-scale building and refurbishment. Conceptually, the municipality wished to provide ample opportunities for small, as well as larger-scale enterprises, to be attracted to the area and generally to maintain, in a renovated state, many of the older significant structures. Nevertheless as a property holder and potential developer in the area, the municipality also has the capacity to commission its own projects and to use its leverage (i.e., with institutions like the universities) to bring further building projects to the area. Among the higher profile undertakings now underway, a largely commercial complex providing some 215,000 square meters of space designed by Manuel de Solà-Morales, promises to make deft and sympathetic use of existing industrial structures and an existing open space on the north-west side of the Diagonal, whereas the audio-visual campus proposed by Winy Maas with Beth Galí brings a new scale and style of building to the area. Eduard Bru's proposal for a high-rise mixed-use complex, parallel to the Rambla de Poblenou has resulted in local controversy, although the massing of building volumes, cross access through blocks and the general streetscape of the proposal, have been carefully handled. In fact, projected property economics and floor space demands within 22@BCN appear to be such that larger volumes, if not densities, will be required.

    Finally, the fourth and furthest along of the projects within the 'triangle' is the Fòrum 2004 – the site for the Universal Forum of Cultures, co-sponsored by the Municipality of Barcelona, the Generalitat and the Spanish Government, in collaboration with UNESCO.[48] There were three core themes for this international gathering of experts, politicians and 'talking heads.' They were: 'cultural diversity,' meaning valuing commonality among people while not losing sight of differences; 'sustainable development,' meaning achieving a balance of development with natural resources, as well as social and economic goods; and 'conditions of peace,' meaning social and political justice through communication and concerns for human rights. It was a 141 day and night event running from the 9th of May to the 26th of September 2004, replete with day and night entertainment, special events, some four permanent exhibits and 49 so-called 'dialogs,' comprising discussions within eleven thematic topical blocks that took stock of what was going on in the world. Special emphasis was placed on European values – a recurrent theme among Barcelona's international expositions and ambitions – this time in the construction of a new world order and the importance of collective memory in paving avenues towards peace. In short, it was another contrivance for Barcelona to occupy a central position on the international stage and officially began, back in July of 2002, with what can only be described as a rumba party with political speeches, that took place on Montjuïc essentially to prepare the population for the forthcoming event, with careful analogies drawn to the Olympic Game's effort and the need to use the opportunity to improve the physical character of the city once again.

The venue for Fòrum 2004 was located at the end of the Diagonal, where it finally meets the sea coast, adjacent to the Besòs River, in a precinct at the end of Rambla de Prim, built partially on land fill, with good access from the Ronda del Litoral and nearby public transportation. A total of approximately 6 hectares in area, the site was mainly parallel to the coastline and consisted of around nine major building components and installations. First, there was the convention center itself and other support facilities, designed by Josep Lluís Mateo – a shiny metal box with angled walls and, with a capacity of some 15,000 persons, the largest convention center in Southern Europe. Straightforwardly rectangular in plan – 150 by 130 meters in dimension – the convention center proper allows for considerable internal flexibility and the angular outer wall surface, covered primarily with perforated metal, alleviates the potential monotony and outsized scale the large building volume might have had otherwise.[49] An expansive well-lit, double-height interior concourse at ground level also makes the building more approachable and intelligible at a pedestrian scale. Ancillary functions, such as shopping, service facilities and a hotel also complement the primary program in a predictable manner. At least economically speaking, the Convention Center also appears to be an unqualified success, being fully booked for the next four years. Second, there was the Fòrum building, flanking the other side of the termination of the Rambla de Prim from the Convention Center. Designed by Herzog and de Meuron, the building – triangular in plan form – accommodates general exhibition space above the ground-floor lobby and passages for pedestrian access through, or rather, under the building. Perceptually, the overall mass of the building, with its irregular, deep-blue 'nubby' surface punctuated irregularly in vertical strips and fragments of reflective glass windows, appears to hover above the paved ground surface. The underside soffit of the building volume was clad in shiny metal panels, which, together with the glazing of the lobby walls and skylit penetrations into the exhibition space above, further reinforced the appearance of a floating mass. At times and in certain places, aspects of the building take on a surreal effect that works on one, often in contradictory manners. From a distance, for instance, the structure seems like a dense, almost-volcanic mass, seeming to be undergoing partial fragmentation. Closer up, especially in juxtaposition with the reflective glazed fragments, this dense mass appears to even push outward into space, with an otherwise implausible sense of levitated density. Third, there was the Esplanada del Fòrum, by Torres and Lapeña, together with adjacent exhibition space, partially forming a platform for the semi-covered plaza and a giant solar array, angled and mounted on concrete pylons, beneath which there is a public viewing platform and further minor exhibition space. At the center of the scheme, an indoor-outdoor system of pergolas and frames for smaller, temporary exhibitions was provided, occupying the higher portion of the Fòrum site, which, incidentally, generally slopes upwards from the Diagonal before becoming a coastal sea wall. Several constructed elements, spreading out from the higher plaza level, appear to be less buildings, per se, than parts of the site's topography, with cubic masses and open stairways forming a sculptured edge to the port lagoon in the direction of Besòs and with enclosed volumes providing for an additional 42,000 square meters of exhibition space.

Surrounding these core conference and exhibition functions, several largely outdoor recreational facilities were or are in the process of being provided. First, there is the Port Esportiu, by David Baena and Toni Casamor, encompassing about 165,000 square meters of constructed multi-use space around the edge of a lagoon, eventually intended as a marina. Second, there is the Parc Litoral Nord-Est at the mouth of the Besòs River, adjacent to the port and to an existing and refurbished power plant, by the firm of Ábalos and Herreros, consisting of additional beach and landscaped areas. Third, there is the Parc Litoral Sud, on the other side of the Fòrum venue, running parallel to the coast, by Farshid Moussavi and Alejandro Zaera-Polo of Foreign Office Architects. Imaginatively formed as part esplanade and part-occupiable park space at a more intimate scale, including several amphitheaters and performance areas, this linear landscape seems to draw, appropriately given its location, on a geomorphic metaphor of dunes and wavescapes. A system of rounded masonry blocks was used to create folding retaining walls and sinuous pathways, beside which were placed densely planted and also often undulating landscape elements. Slanted light stanchions, along major pathways also added to the idea of a windswept, active and yet somehow 'frozen' natural terrain. Fourth, Beth Galí, with BB and GG Architects, designed the Zona de Banys, situated on and parallel to the sea wall and groin infrastructure on the sea front of the overall Fòrum site. Intended as a recreational venue, largely for bathing, the design is relatively low key and relates admirably to both the orientation and larger-order infrastructural condition in which it was placed. Fifth, there is the Passarel·la

Peatonal and Edificio de Capitanía by Ernest Ferrér and Mamen Domingo, forming an active pedestrian connection, by way of an eccentrically-constructed trestle bridge, across the port lagoon, between the Fòrum site and the Parc Litoral Nord-Est. Finally, a marine zoo by Conxita Balcells Associates has been proposed along the coast, back in the direction of central Barcelona, to complete the waterfront improvements.

Overall, the Fòrum venue and its adjacent recreational facilities appear as a quite vast and, at times, windswept landscape. Indeed, apart from the Convention Center and perhaps the adjacent Edifici Fòrum at one corner of the site, the design intentions have been clearly in the direction of topographic elements, rather than buildings and landscapes in a conventional manner, apparently in order to both articulate and constitute a broader constructed landscape. Moreover, by pursuing this tack, city officials have once again placed themselves in something of the vanguard of experimental approaches towards contemporary construction of urban public space, largely seeming to discourage more traditionally-based practices used in the past. At present, because of the sheer newness and incompleteness of the undertaking, it is difficult to tell whether this design commitment will be successful. Certainly, looking out over the construction, it seems like no other place in Barcelona and, at times and for some, has an entirely other worldly and perhaps an unsettling, even dystopic appearance, despite the obvious exuberance of many elements in the general landscape and the intended gaiety of their specific use. This sense of spatio-temporal displacement, towards another place at an indeterminate future time, is further reinforced by some of the surrounding development, which also breaks, rather substantially, in both form and aspect, from prior building in Barcelona. To be sure, time and contingent circumstances in all cities, 'move on,' as it were, raising at least the prospect of new expressive urban responses. Coming all at once and in one locale, however, it can have a rather shocking impact.

In the spirit of public-private cooperation in development, several other projects either have occurred or are occurring in the general neighborhood of the Fòrum venue. As might be expected, given the intensive convention and exhibit function, a number of hotels have been and are being constructed, including the Hotel Princess by Òscar Tusquets, Enrique Albín and Jorge Muñoz, at the very end and corner of the Diagonal. By hugging the edges of the triangular site and through a well-detailed metal and glass facade, varying according to specific conditions along its rise, this elegant tower brings a strongly urban sensibility to the area. Also planned, adjacent to the convention center, is the Centre Geriàtric by Lluís Clotet and Ignacio Paricio, another in a long line of special care and medically-related facilities that have been and continue to be constructed along Barcelona's sea front, including the well-known Hospital de Mar and the new Parc de Recerca Biomèdica de Barcelona being constructed next to it, designed by Manuel Brullet and Albert de Pineda, putting into public use what elsewhere might be the sites for opulent high-rise residential areas. Also, in planning and development is the Àrea Universitària del Fòrum by Eduard Bru, part of the overall government strategy to move the center of gravity of tertiary educational facilities, away from their traditional locations at the other end of the city. Then too, there is the nearby Diagonal Mar development under the auspices of Gerald Hines, the American developer, with its relatively conventional residential towers ringing an unconventional park, designed by Enric Miralles, and the adjacent shopping center and commercial complex, again in a conventional manner by Robert A. M. Stern.

The other major part of the 'River to River Transformations,' as noted earlier, is located in the south and south-west of the city, although also in areas outside of the municipality. Close to the center of Barcelona a plan for restructuring the top hills of Montjuïc has been proposed, finally culminating the city's efforts to fully renovate the hilly outcrop, this time with an ecologically-sensitive landscaped zone for non-intensive recreation. Nearby, below the foothills, the Fira 2000 trade fair site is also being extended and updated with a design by Toyo Ito, who won a limited competition for the improvements. His proposal includes a prominent hotel and office building on the Gran Via Corts Catalanes leading into Barcelona, an auditorium complex, and six sizable pavilions for trade exhibits. Infrastructure improvements are also being considered to more closely link the trade fair with Montjuïc and its 1929 Universal Exposition facilities, that could also be used, in tandem, to increase display and other related capacities. Also along the Gran Via is the new Ciutat de la Justícia of 2002 by David Chipperfield, a closely-packed ensemble of buildings, with common podia and ground-level pedestrian connections – like a piece of a city inside a city – to house 330,000 square meters of new and relocated judicial functions and administrative services. Moreover, long stretches of the Gran Via Corts Catalanes itself are also being replanned to better rationalize traffic circulation; bring more substantial landscape amenity to what has been largely an area of warehousing, industry and other service functions; and to provide a more prominent entranceway into Barcelona. Andreu Arriola and Carme Fiol's proposal for a section of the Gran Via to be transformed into an open yet two-level boulevard has already received considerable attention.[50] Further out of the city, towards and within Llobregat, plans are afoot to extend the airport again in El Prat and to incrementally increase the size of the present cargo and bulk-handling port, including logistical facilities. At the airport, a third runway is to be added, with additional passenger and freight-handling terminals to be constructed on the other side of the present terminals, in order to handle up to 40 million passenger trips per year. At the port, pressures for increased cargo-handling space have been increasing for some time. Between 1993 and 1997, for instance, there was a 51 percent increase in throughput, mainly in general cargo, underlining Barcelona's importance as a transportation and distribution hub on the Mediterranean, but also pointing up short comings in the existing port facilities.[51] Over the same period, the docking of cruise ships doubled, as Barcelona became the preferred first call in the western Mediterranean. This circumstance has also proven to be a boon to the local economy through considerable spending by ship-borne tourists and little by way of a strain on local services. However, one aspect of the public works in the lower delta of the Llobregat River that remains controversial is a proposed re-routing of the inner channel to rationalize neighboring land uses and the occupation of distinctive, if not sensitive, environmental areas. This has met with strong reservations from ecologists and those looking for improved environmental quality.

As mentioned earlier, participation in and initiation of projects by the City of Barcelona, beyond its municipal boundaries has required considerably more consensus building among local governments in the metropolitan area than has occurred in the past. No doubt this has been aided by the 'knock-on effect,' as it were, of Barcelona's earlier successes in physically transforming its physical environment and with considerable international notoriety and success. It has also been enabled by more financial and other resources, now in the hands of neighboring communities, among other things, brought on by larger populations and related economic bases from migration away from Barcelona proper. Meanwhile, within the city, upgrading of the Ciutat Vella continues, under imaginative plans by Joan Busquets and others, seeking extensive renovation through well-defined processes of incremental improvement, local initiative and careful urban block reconfiguration.[52] In particular, the Raval section of the old town with high concentrations of immigrant inhabitants, has recently been receiving considerable attention, including the opening of areas for needed public space like the Rambla del Raval. Rather than a static plan to be built in the historic area towards a prescribed outcome, this orientation towards preservation, conservation and urban upgrading admits the possibility of different outcomes and remains flexible, while also adhering to far-less variant presumptions of environmental quality, building standard and, ultimately, of performance. Generally, the appearance of the Ciutat Vella has improved substantially from as recently as only three to five years ago. It does still harbor, however, a considerable amount of illegal drug trade. Specific projects, like the renovation of the Mercat de Santa Caterina of 1997 to 2005 by Enric Miralles and Benedetta Tagliabue, as well as re-configuration of the Born Market, both including recent archaeological discoveries below the surfaces, further reinforce the city's commitment to re-use of older, historic structures, in addition to new building. The same goes for Richard Roger's proposal for the renovation of the now-defunct Plaça de Toros, again on the Gran Via next to the Plaça Espanya, inactive since 1977, into a multi-use facility capable of augmenting nearby conference and performing spaces, as well as having a complementary ensemble of its own activities. With a partially glazed dome over restoration of parts of the old arena, together with active interconnections between various major levels within the complex, Roger's proposal promises to provide a grand and exciting indoor space for the city, probably on an unprecedented scale.

Too Far, Too Fast?

Judging from what's either already in place or under construction and what's moved substantially through the planning process since the late 1990s, Barcelona has progressed forward towards re-positioning itself within its regional if not global context. Major infrastructural improvements, though overdue and not in place as yet, promise to provide a much stronger and thicker network of linkages and processing facilities necessary to sustain the city as a major, if not the major, transportation and distribution hub in the region and a major center in Southern Europe. The construction and improvement, to an international scale and international audience, of convention and trade venues – probably the largest aggregation in Southern Europe – together with ancillary support facilities like hotels and places of entertainment, also places Barcelona in a more competitive position and both recognizes and anticipates the need to nudge economic production, within the city, further in the direction of the service sector. Likewise, a broadening of the base of cultural urban tourism, through better linkage and accommodation to the outside world, as well as a bolstering of its cultural programs and capitalizing further on the distinctive urban-architectural assets and leisure-time activities available within the city, has made Barcelona a primary European destination. Furthermore, a plethora of different kinds of commercial construction, although somewhat less so in housing, continues to be attractive to outside investment and business re-location, again enabling an economic shift in the direction of the service sector. Also, the city began to move more strategically towards 'new economic' activities and began actively courting markets involved in information technology and related knowledge industries. In addition, there appears to have been no diminution in the perception of Barcelona's chief asset – its high 'quality of life,' along with its good business environment. Indeed, the city is a more attractive place, by these kinds of measures, than it was five or six years earlier. Finally, strong leadership from the top in municipal matters, by now following well-honed administrative and technical procedures, again was successful, or at least by and large accepted, in guiding Barcelona towards yet another or continued re-incarnation of itself as a city. Favorable macro-economic circumstances also came into play, as Spain's economy grew by nearly 19 percent since 1998, around 7 percentage points more than the euro area as a whole.[53]

Between these broad, positively-inclined brush strokes, however, there are several disquieting issues, trends and limitations that might qualify such a rosy picture of Barcelona. Mainly, they concern specific aspects or projects within the city's recent round of transformations, but collectively raise questions about whether Barcelona and its leadership was moving too far and too fast, in some instances; while underestimating circumstances to be overcome for imagined outcomes, in other instances; getting the balance right in further instances; and generally pointing up limits to the process of successive re-invention that Barcelona has embarked upon over the past twenty-five years or so. The case for the 'new economy' and 22@BCN, for instance, seems unlikely to be as successful in the manner that may have been expected originally. Initiated when the world-wide 'dot.com bubble' was still inflated, the city's strategy, nevertheless, ignored or seemed unaware of what have proven to be some of the immutable realities of sustained, successful establishment of centers of information and related high-tech development and application. To be fair, Barcelona and Poblenou is not the only place this seems to have happened. There are as many failures as there are successes elsewhere, in this regard, and as discussed earlier in this chapter. In fact, the 'Silicon Valleys' and Bangalores of this world are rather more the exceptions than the general rule. They have come about by virtue of close proximity and interaction with relevant world-class institutions of higher learning. They have been the recipients of heavy, long-term governmental and industrial support for their programmatic activities, and they have developed, again over time, internal labor and managerial cultures, albeit differently, that are self sustaining, usually with high premiums placed on general environmental ambiance and quality. At the moment, anyway, and into the foreseeable future, Barcelona has few of these virtues or they are only weakly present there. Also, as discussed earlier, 'Silicon Alley' in New York, which served as the model closest to Barcelona, business is far from booming, even with levels of support that are probably higher than those that could be mustered, realistically, in Barcelona. In short, nagging questions remain about the efficacy of there being an operational 'new economy,' as imagined, in Poblenou. Certainly, moves have been made to encourage location and re-location of centers of higher learning in or near the area, stretching the center of gravity of such places from other more established areas in the city. However, is it enough, of the right kind, and of sufficient pre-eminence? Just as certainly, plans have been made and are being carried out to physically transform the area into a variety of commercial, service industry and related residential functions, with a keen eye towards different requirements of would-be investors and tenants, be they small, moderately-sized, or large. However, as the recent history of entrepreneurial aggregations in the so-called 'new economy' have suggested, firms can be highly foot-loose and their terms of locational preference can be unpredictable and even fickle. Somewhat less certain, but a plausible basis for Barcelona's immersion in information technology and related knowledge industries, is its high standing, at least in the Spanish-speaking world, in publishing and related media. However, isn't this already underway and in other parts of the city and metropolitan area? Then, beyond these essentially physical facilitations of 22@BCN, over which the city can rightly exert its energies, there are much larger-order issues, well beyond such influence. Huge amounts of research and development capital, for one, appear to be in a much larger national and international bailiwick, with substantial competition from other claimants. A spontaneous culture of entrepreneurial inclinations of the right kind, for another, does not come readily to Barcelona partially for the reasons described earlier in this chapter. At best, the planned transformation of Poblenou, under the 22@BCN program, should probably be viewed more simply as another urban renovation and renewal of a district and neighborhoods with what that implies, including resistance on the part of locals for what they might construe, at times, as going too far into unnecessary gentrification. It seems unlikely that the projected 130,000 new jobs will turn up any time soon and the recent decision to increase the proportion of residential development does not seem inappropriate, as well as the plans for further public open-space improvements.

Then, there is the venue for Fòrum 2004 and its after use. As mentioned, it is vast and houses a collection of numerous and somewhat specialized facilities for conventions, exhibitions, performances and other large gatherings, in addition to area-wide park and recreational spaces. Its capacity, during the Fòrum, was pegged at somewhere like 40,000 to 50,000 people per day, although that seems even somewhat low, given the size and spatial articulation of the site.

In fact, it never actually reached near that capacity, let alone on a regular basis over the course of a long event.[54] Even recognizing both the need and opportunity to construct an international standard of convention and other related facilities, the issues of size, or expansiveness, and degree of aggregation of facilities, still seems to remain, begging the question of what happens afterwards. Further, although Barcelona is a relatively compact city, as discussed earlier, and avoiding questions about any alternative sites, the venue is perceived by many to be distant from the 'center of things,' so to speak, in the city. While this perception may be only a matter of the present geography and will change over time, once the area becomes more established, remedial action, as required at the site for Seville's World's Fair, may also become necessary to more fully and purposefully integrate the venue into the city. If appropriately managed, the benefits to the nearby neighborhoods in Sant Martí and in Besòs, socially and environmentally marginalized for so long, on the other hand, are likely to become relatively clear and useful.

Further, during this plunge into large capital projects by the city, other issues have also arisen without clear resolutions. On the broader environmental front, atmospheric emissions have continued to rise over the past ten years, as noted earlier. Periodic overloading of treatment plants, through a single rather than double system of pipes, continues to aggravate the danger of continued water pollution. Adequate fresh water resources may also become an issue in the near future. Beyond its immediate control, although within its realm of suasion as the leader in the metropolitan area, the Municipality is and should also be concerned with issues of mobility and sprawl. No doubt there is some resentment towards the city from its neighbors, due to its success and stance within the region, but there is a case to be made for the inevitable fact that 'they are all in much the same boat together,' as it were, and that environmental issues rarely, if ever, stop at political boundaries. Also, substantial immigration, usually of poorer people as in the past, although now from both inside and outside of the Spanish-speaking world, are influencing the city's demography and creating some social and cultural tensions in what is otherwise a reasonably tolerant population. These range from very real strains on services, all the way through to misunderstandings about the accepted way of going about things in daily life. Again this is not peculiar or even particular to Barcelona. Much of Europe is beginning to feel the same tensions and pressures. However, being perceived as being a rich and progressive city, certainly within the Spanish context, can bring with it extra burdens and responsibilities in these regards. In addition, there is rising crime in the city and the quality of education and its relationship to employment opportunities, especially among younger adults, remains a problem, although again also moving beyond the city's immediate remit and resources. Then too, negative perceptions about strong government intervention into the dealings of the private sector have appeared, from time to time, just below the surface of what seems to be an amiable and progressive atmosphere of public-private relations. This may be simply a facet of strong public leadership and all to be good. At those moments, however, when the City needs substantial private sector participation, as in many of the projects now underway, too much paternalism and control can be counter productive. In fact, partly because of some public reaction to this round of large capital projects, among other issues, Mayor Clos and his government received a more qualified mandate from the voters during the 2003 municipal elections, than they enjoyed previously. Although re-elected in coalition, the PSC lost five seats in the council and drew a proportion of the vote that was among the lowest in the socialist party's municipal electoral history. Their rival, the PP, however, and its candidate – Alberto Fernández Díaz – faired little better, gaining just one seat on the council, with the CiU losing a seat. Among other parties that faired well were the 'greens' – *Iniciativa per Catalunya Verds* (ICV) – which gained several seats.[55]

Finally, returning to a point made earlier regarding Barcelona's consistent occupancy of the vanguard on matters of urban-architectural expression, a question can be raised about how extensively this more or less official stance can persist, without running into several outcomes that are less flattering than those that have occurred in the past. Looking back over the 'River to River Transformations,' many of the projects, laudably, have been encouraged to take on different, sometimes seemingly experimental, and even novel forms. Well known as something of a laboratory for urban architecture in contemporary times, as well as at other times, Barcelona, during this recent binge of public projects, continued to set its architectural sights high and wide, but, did it go too far, or is that legitimately even possible to comment on here? The answer is probably yes on both counts, at least from several vantage points, and had little to do with the efforts of the architects involved. On the production side of projects, architects were selected and engaged largely on the basis of limited and invited competitions. Review of projects in process then came before 'quality commissions,' as they were called, for comment, advice and guidance. These procedures were again all to the good. However, they tended to involve a group, often an international group, of like-minded people, who were also knowledgeable, sophisticated and largely open, in a worldly way, to design thinking from elsewhere, as well as locally. Consequently, matters of urban-architectural expression and, indeed, programmatic configuration, were pushed, unconsciously or not, in many contemporary if not avant-garde directions. At times also, a collector's mentality came into play, along with the architectural connoisseurship, leading almost predictably to a certain roster of architects, among others, or less specifically to particular formal pre-projections of projects that might be existing and architecturally interesting to have in the city, although perhaps only for some. In terms of advancing the 'arts' of architecture there is nothing much wrong with this orientation. Problems arise, however, on the reception side of projects, when pushing the proverbial 'urban-architectural envelope' outstrips popular taste or, in a city like Barcelona where this taste is well-developed and often tolerant of contemporaneity in design, when a point of sheer saturation is reached with regard to novelty and enough becomes enough. A similar response also comes about when the public, or when publics, who may be far from 'died-in-the-wool' traditionalists find themselves befuddled, perplexed and estranged by what they see and experience, particularly when the projects involved come, as they do in Barcelona, on the heels of other contemporarily-inclined, public-sponsored efforts in the recent past. As discussed earlier in chapters two and three, it is often difficult to judge, or pre-judge, such a threshold. Comments, for instance, like "I'm not sure where I am any more," or "all this is beginning to look , or looks, like somewhere else," heard, for instance, around the Fòrum, do signal some disquiet, although, from a critical-theoretical point of view, they do also beg the question of whether appearing to be from 'somewhere else' is still a valid projective position to take. It may well be that deeper impetuses behind 'somewhere else' are also present in Barcelona, although without much in the way of architectural revelation. It may also be that a whole program, or set of programs, is new to the city, although logically required in order to move forward and to make better lives for people, bringing with it elements of different scales and expressive strangeness. In both cases, thresholds of acceptance may or may not have been breached, or it is simply a matter of time and sustained acquaintance. One aspect of this kind of discussion is relatively clear, however. When the public becomes largely satisfied with their lot and physical circumstances, having bought into successive rounds of substantial urban-architectural novelty, transformation and even experimentation, they will balk at more that is different. The current situation in Barcelona, surrounding at least some of its new projects, seems to have skirted very close to, if not over, this kind of threshold, raising the very real possibility that the city, while offering strong and otherwise responsible leadership, moved, as it were, 'too far and too fast.'

GONE TO MARKET .... *'the catch of the day, come what may'*

Mercat de Gràcia

Street Shopping

Mercat de Gràcia

Mercat de la Boqueria

Mercat de la Boqueria

Mercat de Santa Caterina

Mercat de Santa Caterina

Zara at Portal de l'Àngel

MEANWHILE, DOWN AT THE FORUM .... *'a brave new world was forming'*

Fòrum and Surroundings

Fòrum explanade

Solar Array

Fòrum Towards Diagonal Mar

Pedestrian bridge and Power Station

Hotel Princess

Fòrum Building

Fòrum Building

EXPANDING VISION

One perceptible way in which a city can change the collective manner in which it is viewed, at least officially, is by altering the focal length of the lens, so to speak, that is used to examine both its problems and opportunities for further development. Not to place overly much credence in efforts at boundary definition around issues of urbanization, for so often they change and shift in unexpected spatial directions, but there is something to be said for radically shifting frames of reference during a city-building process, even if it is only to keep up with the times. Barcelona did this to considerable effect, for instance, during the 1980s, by generally accepting a configuration of the overall spatial envelope in which the city was to operate, and then setting about to narrow its focus – as described earlier in chapter two – in order to address the needs of specific locations with regard to reconstructive activity. Likewise, the opposite focal length – of looking outwards rather than inwards – can have a similar salutary effect and constructive import. For some time now, not least since the preparations for the Olympic Games in 1992, Barcelona has been doing just that, although not necessarily in a thoroughly-organized, official and deliberate manner. Moreover, if anything, this outward orientation by way of both vision and ambition has persistently been the city's preferred orientation. It has allowed Barcelona to address its physical needs and to simply expand as a way of looking beyond Spain and Catalonia in maintaining its economic vitality and sense of independence. Often, within the Spanish context Barcelona has been both described and sought to be the 'north of the south,' implying being part of the nation but also having other important cultural-economic ties elsewhere. Certainly, Barcelona, among largish cities, is not alone in this proclivity, for its not as if 'bragging' and other more tangible rights don't accrue to cities of size in their various national settings, nor that size doesn't often offer considerable advantage by way of both particular and peculiar amenity to city inhabitants, businesses and other interests. Nevertheless, taking up more fully and officially with urbanizing expansiveness and urban restructuring usually takes time. Again from a more or less official planning perspective, it also often places a city in a position of suddenly appearing to be different than it either is or was at some earlier moment in time. Indeed, both of these conditions obtain in Barcelona. But, as in the past, they became the source of a broader more inclusive vision of the city and its essential role in a burgeoning metropolitan region. In addition, part of this becoming, or appearing to be something else, engendered a different sense of significance, importance and pre-occupation with regard to local city building. Today in Barcelona this seems to be occurring again and represents the end of an era in many respects. In effect, a broader regional metropolitan vision, beyond the city itself, is both a respectable and an appropriate way out of past practices and one that potentially offers Barcelona an opening to a new and prosperous future.

Toward Regional Metropolitanism

A useful way to begin exploring dynamics, that have recently shaped Barcelona, is by way of the spatial and jurisdictional circumstances in which the city resides at regional, provincial and metropolitan levels. Barcelona, as often noted earlier, is the capital of the Region of Catalonia – one of 17 regions in Spain, with a population in 1999 of 6,207,533 inhabitants, representing around 16 percent of the national total, and made up of some 944 municipalities of which the City of Barcelona is one. Outside of Spain the region also has strong historical and economic ties with the regions of Languedoc-Roussillon and Midi-Pyrénées, in France, including the cities of Montpellier and Toulouse, respectively. The Province of Barcelona is one of four in Catalonia, very roughly more or less equal in area, the others being Lleida, Girona and Tarragona. The surface area of the Province is 7,728 square kilometers, divided among 310 municipalities, and its population in 1999 was 4,706,325 people, or 76 percent of the regional total. More important for this discussion, the Metropolitan Region of Barcelona is one of five within Catalonia, the others being Lleida, Girona and Tarragona again, and Manresa in the same province. The area of the Metropolitan Region, under current boundary definitions is 3,236 square kilometers, or 42 percent of the Province and the population in 1999 was 4,301,947, or 69 percent of Catalonia's total, and made up of 163 municipalities. Under other regional-metropolitan boundary definitions, to be discussed later, the population rises to 4.4 million inhabitants and to from 218 to 252 municipalities. Besides Barcelona, other major communities within the Barcelona Metropolitan Region include: Sabadell, Terrassa and Martorell, to the north-west, Vilafranca, Vilanova and the various jurisdictions of Llobregat to the south; and Mataró, Badalona and other communities within the Baix and Alt Maresme, as well as Granollers and Sant Celoni to the north-east. The Metropolitan Area of Barcelona covers an area of 585 square kilometers with 2,908,789 inhabitants in 1999, roughly twice the municipality's population and around 64 percent of the Metropolitan Region's total, and now incorporates 30 municipalities, including the 27 that were part of the General Metropolitan Plan of 1976. Then, moving further down in geographic scale there is what is known as the Barcelona Conurbation, including the city and several tiers of some 13 surrounding communities, with an area of 223 square kilometers. Finally, the City of Barcelona has an area of 99 square kilometers and a population, again in 1999, of 1,503,451 inhabitants. Apart from the arcaney of this spatial description, which grows in part from past county and municipal boundary drawing by the regional government, a depiction merges of an expansive urbanized area extending geographically well beyond its primary center in the City of Barcelona into other nearby concentrations of population in largish communities, but generally with increases in overall urban density. The current density of the City of Barcelona, for instance, is around 15,170 people per square kilometer, whereas the comparable figure for the Barcelona Metropolitan Region is only around 1,330 people per square kilometer. In fact, Barcelona is a relatively dense city by world standards, although as a region it is not, with population densities dropping off sharply, apart from the nearby communities, once one moves beyond the Barcelona Conurbation. Within the broader context of Catalonia, the Barcelona Metropolitan Region is also dominant, accounting massively for about 84 percent of the metropolitan regional population within Catalonia's five major centers.[1] It also dwarfs the populations of Toulouse, Montpellier and Nîmes, across the French border and currently ranks sixth, as noted earlier in chapter four, within the European community, only slightly outstripped in Spain by Madrid.

Catalonia remains one of Spain's economic powerhouses on the regional level, although again as noted earlier not with the same superiority that it enjoyed in the past. In fact, its GDP per capita, on a basis of 1986 equaling 100 on a scale of relative performance, shifted from 140 in 1995 to 157 in 2000, during Spain's recent economic recovery, whereas the same measure for Madrid went from 130 to a comparable level, around 160, in the same year.[2] Also, a recent study showed that between 1995 and 2002 Catalonia ranked fourth in productivity, at around 2.4 percent per annum, behind Madrid which headed the list, followed by Pais Vasco and Navarra. This compares to Spain with an overall figure of 0.6 percent per annum, but around 3 percent between 2000 and 2003.[3] Further data for GDP per capita, only this time at purchasing power parity, also show Catalonia lagging behind Madrid and well behind, for instance, Lombardia and Piemonte in Italy, two of Europe's richer areas, at least within a Mediterranean scheme of things.[4] Net flows of capital, on the other hand, significant economic drivers, remain net positive in Catalonia, while the opposite is the case in Madrid, although outflows from Catalonia have accelerated since 1998.[5] Overall the region's sectoral mix of economic activity has modernized appreciably, now standing at 58 percent in services, 29 percent in industry, 10 percent in construction and 3 percent in agriculture, once the dominant aspect of the economy.[6]

Barcelona and its metropolitan region is, however, where Catalonia's economic prowess sharpens and where many, although not all, comparisons move in the opposite direction. Barcelona is Spain's leading industrial and commercial city and the metropolitan pivot of the northwestern Mediterranean, extending as far as Marseilles in France. It accounts for over 10 percent of Spain's economic added value, and ranks fifth in exports in Europe, well ahead of Madrid and other Spanish metropolitan areas. In fact, the surface area in the Barcelona metropolitan area devoted to economic activity exceeds that of Madrid by at least ten percent, with almost double the amount devoted to industry.[7] As such, it is the export springboard of Spain, accounting for 22.3 percent of total exports in goods and agricultural products, rising from 20.5 percent before the recent economic growth began during the second quarter of 1994. This is well in excess of Madrid's exports, at 10.9 percent of Spain's total, and the gap appears to be widening.[8] Moreover, technology is playing an increasing role in Barcelona's production and throughput, with medium-to-high technology amounting to 63 percent of its value of exports, up from 59 percent in 1988, and with an extensive expansion in trade coverage, up from 28 percent to 60 percent over the same period. Indeed, certainly over the past ten years, Barcelona has become less dependent upon the Spanish economy, due largely to more aggressive entry into European and other foreign markets. Also, at present, measures of comparative advantage, among varying degrees of technology within Barcelona's regional-metropolitan industries, favor high technology, well ahead of both medium-high and medium-low intensities. Overall, however, there also appears to be considerable room for further growth in higher technological content in production, if the metropolitan region is to remain competitive. Similar to Catalonia, a little more than 60 percent of Barcelona's metropolitan economic activity is in the tertiary sector and the metropolitan region maintains a strong manufacturing base. Per capita incomes are around 150 percent of figures for Spain and higher than European norms, as noted in chapter four.

Unlike metropolitan areas in the United States and many other parts of Europe, the average sizes of businesses in the Barcelona metropolitan region are small, similar in sizes to those in Japan and in Italy, at least in manufacturing, although not in services like finance and insurance, where sizes in Japan and Italy tend to be higher.[9] To be sure, there has been a world-wide metropolitan trend towards smaller average sizes of businesses. However, some of the numerical differences are striking. Overall, the average size of businesses in New York City and Philadelphia within the United States, are around 18 and 28 employees, respectively, with the metropolitan region of Barcelona registering around ten employees and the city around four employees. In manufacturing, the comparisons are much the same, with Barcelona at around thirteen employees and London, for instance, at around 29 and with Chicago at around 55 employees. Finance and insurance, one of Barcelona's regional strong suites, is perhaps even more striking, with around eleven employees, far less even than a comparable city like Milan, in Italy, with around 36 staff members and the Japanese – comparable overall – with around 20 and above employees.[10] Setting aside which arrangement is actually better than another, for the firms concerned presumably remain more or less competitive, these size differences can be put down to relatively high levels of networking, flexibility, synergy and complementary activity among businesses. In Barcelona, these businesses also seem to enjoy specific economies of location and of agglomeration, including social cohesion, as well as having other helpful amenities near at hand within a sizeable metropolis. A little like the so-called 'industrial districts' of northern and central Italy, discovered during the late 1970s although mooted earlier, smallness of individual firm size need not mean lower overall production from a specific region or territory, even though some contradictory interpretations have also emerged about the northern and central Italian phenomenon.[11]

Spatially and economically, the portrait of Barcelona's metropolitan region that emerges is of a large multi-centered metropolis, encompassing numerous municipalities, with constituent centers providing necessary specialization within an otherwise diverse manufacturing and service base. In many ways, matters of sheer scale aside, this is a similar picture of metropolitan development to be found elsewhere in the world, such as in the United States since the 1970s. In Barcelona's region, there are, for instance, regional concentrations of particular kinds of industries, like textile and garment making in Sabadell, Terrassa and Mataró. There are also strong networked relationships between and among cities, such as at Granollers and its hinterland where services are shared. Moreover, there are higher levels of specialization occurring in the City of Barcelona itself in tertiary services and especially among real-estate and corporate financial enterprises. Further, recent scholarship shows that this multi-centered format is also a historical feature of the region since at least the late sixteenth and early-seventeenth centuries and, therefore, is deeply ensconced.[12] Added to this,

Barcelona is large, but not too large. It also enjoys, as noted several times in this text, high qualities of life and the less tangible values which flow from this by way of creativity, personal fulfillment and business potential. No doubt as something of a consequence of this rosy portrait, Barcelona posted a gain of 150,000 jobs, between 1995 to 2000, more than making up for the loss of around 100,000 jobs during the post-Olympic downturn and malaise described earlier in chapter three. The Barcelona metropolitan region, on the other hand, over the same duration, created 240,000 jobs, probably a better measure of Barcelona's economic progress, and one that further shifts the emphasis in the direction of a larger catchment area of economic activities.[13]

Moving from portraiture to 'moving pictures,' so to speak, the spatial dynamics of Barcelona's metropolitan region, and the city's new role within it, are also bound up with infrastructure, especially with regard to present and future urban management and city building. Continuing in an economic vein for a moment longer, as the market for goods and services produced in the Barcelona Metropolitan Region has grown, so too has the geographical area that forms an integral part of the region's economy. Moreover, it extends well beyond the official limits considered by the Barcelona Metropolitan Regional Plan, especially in conjunction with the spatial spread towards Tarragona, Manresa and Girona, that has occurred strongly since 1991. Quite probably, Barcelona's metropolitan market will expand to 4.8 million inhabitants in the not too distant future, with a commuting area covering over 80 percent of Catalonia's population.[14] Even with substantial growth among Catalonia's other four metropolitan regions, Barcelona still accounts for about 85 percent of all employment – a 50 percent expansion between 1986 and 1996, with only a 22 percent increase in population. Further, this trend also shows a strengthening of the central municipality – the City of Barcelona – with regard to the rest of the metropolitan region. Statistically, all the metropolitan regions in Catalonia show declines in the rates of employment to populations, since 1986, moving largely from a 1:3 or 1:4 range (i.e., the number of employees per population) to a 1:2 or 1:3 range. Girona and Tarragona, closely linked to Barcelona, posted the most impressive employment gains, at 71 percent and 74 percent over the ten year period between 1986 and 1996, on population gains of 55 and 42 percent, respectively.[15] Certainly, part of those shifts can be accounted for by lower natural growth rates and higher participation in the work force. Nevertheless, they are also expressive of economic vitality and strength within the region, even if unemployment, although much lower than the earlier 1990s, remains relatively high in comparison to some European and American counterparts.[16]

Recently, the spatial distribution of urban and economic growth, within the Metropolitan Region of Barcelona, has been marked by the influence of nodes, or poles, of activity and by growth corridors between traditional and new centers. Again, this simply highlights the further transformation of the region of Barcelona into a multi-centric terrain with strong links, including development in between, not unreminiscent of similar spatial forms of development, again in the United States, other parts of Europe and, very recently, in places like China in East Asia, where the Changjiang Delta immediately comes to mind.[17] Strong nodes of economic and related development in the Barcelona region have occurred around Terrassa, Sabadell and especially around and within Martorell. Strong corridors of development have sprung up along major highways, like the Martorell corridor, roughly paralleling the Llobregat River, and within the ring and radial road system of the first tiers of municipalities surrounding the City of Barcelona. Furthermore, the location of larger industrial enterprises, perhaps less of a rarity than the previous discussion of the sizes of business firms might belie, has also tended to favor roadway corridors between major centers. All of this should come as no surprise. Again based on experience in other settings, link-node spatial configurations of development, within an otherwise urbanizing territory, are hardly uncommon. Moreover, large new industrial and related plants, per force of cheaper extensive land areas with good transportation access, tend to proliferate along major roadways away from more highly-developed and, therefore, more expensive urban property. Given present-day commuting patterns, they can also afford to be more footloose than they might have been in the past, tied down to particular sources of labor. Further, independent re-location of skilled labor forces on urban peripheries, or in neighboring metropolitan towns for space and life-style reasons, further reinforces this trend. In the center of the metropolitan region itself, both in response and in anticipation of this out-migration and re-location of industry, a conversion to higher-level, knowledge-based service activities has also been occurring, shifting the focus away from earlier manufacturing. Indeed, this was part of the underlying logic for the 22@BCN redevelopment exercise in Poblenou, one of Barcelona's old industrial cores discussed in chapter four.

A key ingredient in this form of multi-centric, link-node, regional territorial development is the possibility and enablement of substantial commuting between and among municipalities and economic centers. Statistics for the number of commuters making trips between municipalities only in the Metropolitan Region of Barcelona, showed a strong upward trend from 386,745 in 1986 to 655,681 in 1996, or almost a doubling in ten years. Moreover, the number of connections between municipalities rose from 6,638 to around 9,700 over the same period, with most of the commuter trips made in private vehicles. Those employed since 1996 have increased by around 30 percent, while the growth in commuting has outstripped this proportional figure. More specifically, there has been a fall in commuting by those employed in their own municipality, from around 65 to 55 percent and a corresponding increase in those commuting beyond their municipality up to 10 minutes away, and an even larger increase – from 17 percent to 23 percent – for those commuting up to 20 minutes away. In short, there has been a general decline in those working in their own municipality compared to those either forced, or willing, to commute. One measure of the social cost of this commuting is the time spent per journey which rose, on average between 1986 and 1996, from around 13.5 minutes to 14.3 minutes.[18] When compared to commuting times in some other cities, such as Atlanta or Los Angeles in the United States, these estimates may seem relatively trivial. However, in the Barcelona metropolitan region there has also been a significant rise in the number of longer commutes, within the 25 to 45 minute range, more comparable with those in the above-mentioned American cities, and this trend seems likely to continue.

In the push and pull between residential and employment locations, that this sort of reconfiguration of urbanizing territory sets off, the City of Barcelona lost some 200,000 inhabitants between 1986 and 1998, as mentioned in chapter four, while the first metropolitan tier of surrounding municipalities, mainly made up of dormitory communities serving the city, lost around 55,000 inhabitants. The metropolitan corridors leading out from the city into the metropolitan region, by contrast, gained around 165,000 inhabitants, and the outlying cities, which began functioning as economic growth poles, gained a further 56,000 people. In addition, less dense, yet attractive cities in the second metropolitan tier, outside of the City of Barcelona, increased by around 74,000 people.[19] In essence, there was a decentralized re-shuffling of population within the metropolitan region, again well-known elsewhere in the world, where what amounts to about 255,000 inhabitants left the central city and its environs, whereas somewhat more (i.e., around 295,000 inhabitants) moved into other regional metropolitan areas, either through re-location, or as newcomers. Again, as discussed in chapter four, part of the reason for this outward migration was affordability of larger residential space standards, as well as associated environmental amenities, in addition to proximity to places of employment.

Unfortunately, the environmental impact of this reshuffling has been less than propitious, moving, for some, to unsustainable levels if continued. Urban sprawl has once again raised its proverbial head, around what was an otherwise compact and relatively dense urban conurbation with a relatively minimal environmental footprint. Moreover, less than well-regulated peripheral development in search of amenable sites has caused water pollution and land-resource problems. Adequate municipal servicing has become more difficult and costly, as urbanization spreads and densities of development become sparse. Most of the dramatic rise in commuting, as discussed earlier, requires the use of private automobiles, resulting in increased mobile sources of atmospheric emissions and use of fossil fuels. Further, the spatial patterns of sparser peripheral developments, as elsewhere in the world, together with widely dispersed commuter patterns, are more difficult to adequately service with public transportation than their denser, less spatially-separated counterparts. Ecosystem damage, through inadequate urban planning and indiscriminate occupation, has also begun to threaten natural habitats and other natural ecological features, within and around the expanding metropolitan region.[20]

If anything, several major infrastructural projects, already in play, will further fuel the multi-centric, diverse, yet spatially-specific and often specialized spatial pattern of urban and economic activity within the Barcelona metropolitan region. There are the airport and port expansions, discussed in chapter four as part of the 'River to River Transformations' of Barcelona, together with associated highway and rail links improving access. To be sure, these will likely promote further economies of agglomeration having a positive effect, generally, on most activities. There is also the high-speed railway link to Madrid and also on into France, that will likely have a similar effect of positioning Barcelona more strongly in its region and internationally, with concomitant impacts in many other places within the metropolitan region. In addition, there are also plans for another – fourth – ring road, likely to thicken the urban network already in place within the region, again with further both centralizing and decentralizing effects of the kind already underway.[21] Then, there is the matter of freight rail transport, already being hotly contested with Madrid, at least with regard to route alignments, as there is general agreement on the need for network improvement. At present, about 4 percent of all freight travel by rail, compared to around 18 percent in other European nations, like Holland and Switzerland, and considerably more in the United States.[22]
The situation is further complicated by the difference in the gauge of track used in Spain compared to the rest of Europe. In the debate over new route alignments connecting into the French freight system, there are at least two alternatives: an alignment traveling north from Madrid through Aragon; and a route traveling

through Barcelona connecting to Toulouse and to Lyon. Of the two, the link through Barcelona seems to be superior from a cost-benefit perspective, but it also challenges the essential centrism of Madrid's infrastructure network models, quite apart from its effect on furthering regional links to French provinces already with a shared cultural history with Catalonia. Much closer to home, proposals are also being examined to create a denser metro-commuter rail network in Barcelona's regional metropolitan area. Some 50 kilometers of subway are being planned and are partly under construction to extend the total available network to around 135 kilometers, over the next ten years.[23] Less conspicuous, in this transportation mix, are buses – apparently not very popular, even though Madrid has about twice the bus network of Barcelona. Inter-modality in transportation, where one switches from one system to another through, for example, 'park and ride' facilities, have also not gained much ground in Barcelona. Indeed, for advocates of this latter approach to decrease time and congestion costs, parking in Barcelona has probably been made too easy.

Further articulation of Barcelona's metropolitan region as a diverse, multi-centered, nimble and competitive business environment will come – probably of necessity – by way of further shifts into a knowledge-based economy. As noted earlier in this section, measurement of present competitive advantage among Barcelona's industries with varying technological content, already favors those with higher intensities. In addition, pursuit of a knowledge-based economy moves beyond simply the appearance of information and communication's technologies, or the arrival of the Internet, into careful identification of sectors and sub-sectors with competitive advantages and then the appropriate use of knowledge-based ways for harnessing resources and co-ordinating activities. As a result, the transformations that occur may not appreciably alter the broad sectoral profile of Barcelona's economy (i.e. what is produced) but change the manner in which firms go about their business (i.e., how they produce).[24] In an effort to move Barcelona along in the direction of more sophisticated knowledge-based platforms, with potentially strong economic repercussions, the city has already encouraged location of new university facilities away from traditional locations, with the siting, as discussed in chapter four, of Barcelona University's campus and Pompeu Fabra University's biomedical campus near the venue for Fòrum 2004. However, the educational stock accumulated by Barcelona's citizens, in terms of level, degree and diversity of specialization, etc., is still 30 percent below European levels. Research and development spending is around half what it should be, when compared to Barcelona's international economic and cultural standing, even though it is the highest in Spain.[25] In addition, dispersal of access to knowledge-based infrastructure and operations to other centers within the metropolitan region has only just begun, and further promotion of knowledge-based activities will require careful nurturing of networks and concomitant fostering of economies of agglomeration.

In summary, then, over the past decade and more, the regional metropolitan circumstances of Barcelona have changed significantly and appear to continue shifting. To reiterate, in the process Barcelona and its broad surroundings have become a contemporary, multi-centered, somewhat sprawling, somewhat locally specialized, better connected, agglomeration of communities, or what some might call a 'post-modern metropolis.' Also during the process of these re-arrangements, the metropolitan region has enjoyed and continues to enjoy significant economic success. No doubt furtherance of its competitive position will require significant additional investments and imagination, although, again to reiterate, it is now less dependent upon the Spanish economy than it has been in the recent past and more broadly visible on the international stage. The spatial results of this recent expansion and reshuffling of population and industry have also been dramatic, altering the role to be pursued advantageously among municipalities and constituent centers of activity, including the City of Barcelona. These results also reveal new logics behind settlement phenomena, although not so dissimilar from other emerging metropolises elsewhere in the world. Largely, they came about through an interplay of many actions, in both the public and private sectors, that sought to exploit advantages of location, changing agglomerations of scale, intrinsic or historic competencies, and shifts in technology across a broadening territory.

Preserving Competitive Advantages

From this and other similar accounts, the regional metropolis of Barcelona would seem to be heading towards a bright future and, indeed, problems notwithstanding, this may well be the case. However, up through at least the early 2000s, these accounts are at considerable odds with official ideas and doctrines about the concept of a metropolis, including the General Regional Plan for Catalonia and the Partial Plan for the Barcelona Metropolitan Region, that were based largely on earlier traditional models of economic and regional spatial activity.[26] One of the early cornerstones of this traditional thinking goes as far back as the Regional Plan of 1932, briefly described in chapter one. Commensurate with political, economic and related transportation conditions at the time, this plan favored an isolationist stance, that simultaneously supported a self-sufficient economy less likely to be seriously subject to foreign trade fluctuations. Accordingly, the Catalan government, controlled by Republicans, drew up county and regional jurisdictional boundaries that reflected this local regional perspective, and they have remained largely intact during the present era. Today, a problem for well-coordinated municipal and regional management, as well as for planning, arises when urban metropolitan-wide urbanizing and economic phenomena spill outside of those boundaries. In fact, as described by the statistics presented in the earlier section, this is what has occurred. The more or less spatially-contiguous, reasonably integrated network of cities, constituting Barcelona's metropolitan region in a singular, representative analytical sense, has moved and continues to move beyond the official boundaries of the Barcelona Metropolitan Region. Not only, but so do other metropolitan regions like Tarragona and Girona. Rationally, metropolitan cities, including their closely associated spatial networks of communities, should be the primary unit of planning and governance. More fundamentally, however, the model behind the regional plans is also at odds with the 'facts on the ground,' so to speak. It embodied the idea of highly centralized metropolitan areas amid a hierarchically organized set of lesser locations, in which the primary role of the center – in this case the City of Barcelona – was to produce most of the goods and provide most of the jobs.[27] Moreover, the planning and regulation which followed relied on relatively static perceptions of urban form following function, more or less in a completely identifiable and predetermined manner. As the situation now stands, these ideas, or this basic conceptualization, is no longer valid, even if it might have been earlier. Certainly, the propitious role of the City of Barcelona within the regional metropolitan area, has changed appreciably to one that concentrates on high-end services and on associated logistics. The hierarchical organization of cities and communities has given way to urban networks and interactions, differently construed, within territorial space. Also, economies of agglomeration, along the lines of a city as some immense production machine, have given way to more flexible, selective and knowledge-based interpretations, as well as amenity-based construals. Again, the local-regional centrism of traditional approaches can be viewed more sympathetically against the broader political backdrop of perceived needs, at least within the recent Generalitat, for continuing pressure and orientation towards forms of Catalanism and regional autonomy. Also, their expanded notions of geography, with regard to the rest of Europe, rarely went beyond Languedoc-Roussillon and the Mid-Pyrénées in France, all, historically anyway, somewhat in the thrall of ideas about the Catalan peoples.[28] Nevertheless, for the Barcelona region in this present day and age of broader international engagement and intense competition, such sympathies are far less useful than they once might have been.

In response to these inconsistencies and downright discrepancies, one might be tempted to say, so what? If the metropolitan region of Barcelona is chugging along under its own proverbial steam, as it seems to be, why worry about all the jurisdictional, bureaucratic and planning niceties? Well, a rather big question remains. Is the present situation as good as it can get, and is it, over time, sustainable? To which the answer seems to be no on both counts. Movement into knowledge-based economic activity, where Barcelona's comparative advantage seems to lie, is relatively new and must be fully harnessed on a regional scale and within other communities, if it is to be fully realized. Moreover, inherent competitive advantages of different locales must also be exploited. Transportation and communication linkages, discussed at some length in previous sections, remain relatively sparse, underdeveloped, or still in the planning stages. Natural resource and environmental issues, associated with sprawling urbanization and industrialization within the region, have also mounted, as noted earlier, and the negative effects and broadening environmental footprint of daily commuting and an over dependence on private-automobile use are also growing larger. Also, potential synergies in service delivery and economic co-operation among communities within the region have yet to be fully tapped, if even more thoroughly considered. Fundamentally, the style of regional planning must change if it is to have relevance to what is actually occurring in the metropolitan region. For instance, it must make more out of the nascent pattern of 'industrial district development', perhaps along the lines of the Dutch Randstat or Emilia Romagna in Italy. Similarly, appropriate arrangements of subsidiarity must be sought in order to achieve better economies of scale in service delivery and related synergies among communities and enterprises.[29] Fundamentally, higher and different levels of co-ordination among provincial, regional and metropolitan tiers and units of government will be required, particularly with regard to organization and administration away from fixed geographical categories, as the real extent of the functioning metropolitan region changes, and as the locus of issues needing to be attended there also involve different spatial logics and boundary definitions.

Then too, there are relations with Madrid and the central government that will need to become more sympathetic, particularly with regard to major joint-infrastructural projects and other major investments, if the region is to maximize support for its broader metropolitan project. Over the past ten years, for instance, public infrastructure investment, usually involving participation by central government agencies, has declined appreciably on a per capita basis.[30] General Spanish government investment in poorer regions in the nation, though perhaps laudable from the standpoint of helping those in most need by redistributing public wealth, has frequently been regarded in Catalonia and in Barcelona, as being excessive. In fact, economic logic, *ceteris paribus* would seem to argue for higher investment in the region. It is ranked around fifth or sixth in Europe and is, therefore, a flagship in Spain's modernization and global position and yet it is ranked around 100th in items of necessary infrastructure, like rail stock, on which it's and, by implication, the nation's prominence might depend. High investment in Latin America from Spain, rather than in local situations, although now falling off, also added to the disparity between regional needs and available support. To be sure, gaining external public support for continued development is a political matter and one that cuts both ways – a perennially recurring theme in Barcelona's and Catalonia's history with regard to Madrid and to Spain. Although often receiving necessary support from Catalan interests and members of the CiU during their first term, Aznar's center-right national government had less need during their second term and made little secret of their disdain for regional 'nationalism,' no doubt prompted primarily by Basque separatism, but also 'rubbing off,' so to speak, on Catalonia.[31] This attitude, also coincided with centralist views on many other matters and, as outlined in the previous discussion, a build up of strong, private-sector interests, concentrated in Madrid.

Recently, a political case for another view of Barcelona, its region and, indeed, much of Catalonia, that was less dualistic in its inherent interdependence with Madrid, began to be advanced by Pasqual Maragall and the socialists. Having narrowly lost his initial electoral battle with Pujol and the CiU for the Generalitat in 1999, Maragall and his colleagues went into focused rehearsal for the next contest and set up a shadow arrangement, with regard to Provincial government, in their offices within the Parlament de Catalunya in the Parc de la Ciutadella. A guiding principle in their deliberations was selective decentralization within the Spanish political, social and economic context, which they noted had already been favored as early as the 1960s by the World Bank. A core idea was to optimize Spain as a socio-political and economic network, rather than concentrating on issues of regional identity and unification, and to thoroughly promote Barcelona's and the region's inherent position in the unfolding 'mapping,' as Maragall put it, of that network.[32] By clearly articulating the advantages of this conceptual approach for Spain, as well as for the region, old antagonisms between Barcelona and Madrid would potentially have less political traction and could be set aside. At least in theory this seemed possible. Further, Maragall viewed Europe as a group of cities that could be explained as a system and as a virtual competitive market, as well as through a language that would address both collective and distinct qualities of service, in order to lift standards of provision and urban environmental amenity accordingly. For him, the idea of "the network was the next way forward," or as he put it for Barcelona ... "the network is the way out of being a capital every fifteen years," with obvious reference to the constant prior need for opportunistic events to move the city and its region along and to garner international recognition.[33] Certainly, this was and remains a rather radical, if abstract, re-think of Barcelona and its region, moving even beyond many of the spatial dynamics that are already in play, if not yet fully recognized by municipal and other authorities. At the time, the very concept of metropolitan region implied was more broadly interconnected and defined than narrower spatial definitions, if not ambitions, expressed by others like Mayor Joan Clos, for instance, who were, to be fair, probably viewing the issue of regionalization from the more parochial vantage point of their constituencies. In fact, at the moment there is a continuing discussion among Clos and his colleagues at city hall over the most appropriate scale for the Barcelona Metropolitan Area, within the broader regional context. For them an entity on the order of 600 square kilometers in area and of around 3 million in population seems to be politically manageable and tractable. The contrast with the more extensive and more populous region, as both a discernable and viable economic set of circumstances, only underlines the practical difficultly faced in reaching overlapping consensus on the timing and magnitude of Barcelona's present and future influence.

By 2000, at much the same time as this broad conceptual thinking about Barcelona's strategic place in the world was taking place, Barcelona Regional – Barcelona's technical group for metropolitan planning – was placed under the redoubtable Josep Acebillo, who as noted earlier in chapter four, was also serving as the Chief Architect of the City of Barcelona and had served earlier, under Maragall, in the city's Olympic building organization, among other activities. This group immediately set about to re-examine the Barcelona Metropolitan Region and its broader context with the aim of not so much creating a unitary master metropolitan plan, as in the past, but of developing data bases, information-handling capacities and analyses that could be used to co-ordinate and rationally assist separate municipalities and other authorities in their planning efforts, as well as to guide major intra-regional infrastructure projects, urban-regional economic developments, and urban-environmental policies. Indeed, given the important spatial dynamics now in play, the whole idea of an inevitably static conceptualization of the metropolitan area and region, through a master plan, is less and less appealing. External consultation was also organized on a variety of topics, both for the purposes of understanding better how the metropolitan region was actually functioning and might be better depicted, together with proposals for its orchestration and management. For example, Joan Trullén, from the Department of Applied Economies at the Autonomous University of Barcelona, led a study of regional economics and related issues, resulting in, among other information, *The Barcelona Region and Its Network of Cities: Towards a Compact City*, of October 2000.[34] The thrust of this and other work was also directed towards a clear articulation of spatial principles that might be pressed forward, consonant with the broad idea of a better networked arrangement of places and locations. Indeed, which came first – Maragall's political conceptualization of a 'way out' for Barcelona or related academic ideas – is probably a moot point, given the close alliance, that had existed for some time, between those in government and especially within the Ajuntament and those in the universities. Under the broad canopy of the 'intellectual left' in Barcelona, many had also been trading places, since shortly after the fall of the Franco regime, as noted earlier.

Formed on January 1, 1994, Barcelona Regional followed on the success of IMPUSA – the Municipal Department for Development and Planning, described in chapter three in conjunction with the Olympic projects. In fact, as the planning and developmental obligations of the Olympic effort were completed and phased out by 1993, Barcelona Regional was created in much the same image as IMPUSA. Today the board of Barcelona Regional is chaired by Joan Clos – the Mayor of Barcelona – with Acebillo as the chief executive, supervising a technical staff of some 60 persons. Other partners are also incorporated into the institution's structure, including representatives from central government agencies, like the airport authority, the port authority, the authority for food and markets, and the rail authority, as well as from other more local public agencies. Institutionally, Barcelona Regional is a non-profit, public, technical consultancy, legally able to engage in supra-municipal projects. In effect, it undertakes commissions funded by individual municipalities, like the City of Badalona in connection with development around rail links, as well as studies of a broader geographic nature, like infrastructural strategies for all of Catalonia. Unusual if not unique in the Spanish context,

Barcelona Regional has been the target of legal challenge, resolved in its favor largely because of the essentially broad public nature and transparency of its undertakings, its possession of authoritative and comprehensive information about the region, and the quality of support rendered to various public agencies. A good example of this support can be illustrated by the recent pre-architectural planning of the complicated Sagrera station complex described in chapter four. There a physical planning proposal was developed to a high degree of spatial and developmental resolution involving issues of infrastructural alignment, engineering structure and building massing, as well as institutional co-ordination. In fact, this capacity to give substantial technical definition and guidance to public projects before they enter into subsequent architectural and public-private or private developmental phases of eventual resolution and realization, was a hallmark of IMPUSA, well demonstrated, for instance, by input into the planning of Vall d'Hebron and the Rondes during the Olympic Game's preparations. It is also a hallmark of Barcelona Regional's activities. At the moment, direct involvement by the Generalitat in Barcelona Regional, as a partner with much the same commitment as the City of Barcelona, is being strongly mooted, no doubt due to better relations across the Plaça Sant Jaume and the importance of regional-metropolitan planning to both constituencies.[35] Although the Mayor of Barcelona seems likely to continue chairing the board under this new arrangement, in different political circumstances the leadership, orientation and even present existence of Barcelona Regional may also be expected to change or at least come into contention. If nothing else, such potentialities illustrate the possible fragility of such special authorities, especially when they begin to span very broad constituencies and technical functions. Earlier experience with the formation of some metropolitan authorities in the United States, for instance, ultimately failed in these regards.

Returning to Barcelona Regional's planning efforts, international experts were also engaged, again with an eye towards identifying and exploring underlying spatial principles for regional organization, although the real impact of these undertakings remains to be seen. Richard T.T. Forman, for instance, a professor at Harvard University's Graduate School of Design and one of the pioneers of landscape ecology, undertook a comprehensive study of the Barcelona region, viewing it as a complex mosaic of land uses, surface covers, habitats, and so on, linked by movements of people, animals, water, energy, nutrients and other elements. Completed in early 2003 and published in 2004 as *Mosaico Territorial para la Región Metropolitana de Barcelona*, Forman's study examined the region's landscape and ecological patterns and made recommendations about ways of protecting the inherent systems that were working, while improving the performance of those that were not.[30] Moreover, rather than coming at the subject from the standpoint of preservation at all costs and stopping urban development, Forman and his study advocate the nurturing of natural and related cultural resources so that they improve, despite further urban growth and development. Well received at metropolitan and local levels, the study now forms a key reference in what Acebillo – now Barcelona's Commissioner for Infrastructure and Urbanism and a proponent of this work – describes as ... "dealing with the complexity of balancing growth and natural resources and finding synergies between both." Others like Edward Soja, the internationally-renowned geographer, were also consulted on matters of economics and regional spatial arrangements and networks, although again the real impact remains to be seen. In addition, in-house expertise at Barcelona Regional was also established on several topics and manners of data handling and analysis. For instance, sophisticated techniques for performing fine-grained-environmental analyses of various infrastructure and land-use proposals were developed, including searching for optimum routes for major roads and railways.

Meanwhile, during the regional elections late in 2003, Maragall and the socialists wrested the Generalitat away from the conservative Catalan 'nationalists,' dominated by the CiU, although it took the combined efforts of all those on the left. In fact, the PSC lost votes, by some 6.6 percent, much the same as the CiU. The big winners were the ERC – *Esquerra Republicana de Catalunya* – and to a lesser extent the ICV or 'Greens.'[37] Effectively this meant that there was little diminution of Catalan nationalism, as the ERC seem to favor full independence from Spain. It merely shifted to the left and the governing coalition could yet prove to be problematic for Maragall. Nevertheless, for the first time in their contemporary history, Barcelona and Catalonia were both governed by leadership from the same political party and, as often happens in such cases, with a co-mingling of ambitions, agendas and personalities. The Generalitat has already begun to move on proposals for redefining the Barcelona region based on the earlier period of rehearsal and technical reconsideration, if not in strictly jurisdictional terms, then certainly in the way resources are engaged around networked communities and a reconceptualization of regional metropolitanism. Large-scale infrastructure improvements have received a new impetus and matters of subsidiarity and inter-governmental co-ordination placed firmly on the proverbial conference table. Although vitally important to the continued prosperity of the region, there is not quite the same pre-occupation with the City of Barcelona, or that it should have to go it alone as it did so often in the past. Consequently, the very idea of Barcelona, as a place or a space, has begun to take on a broader and perhaps fuzzier definition, at least for the time being, depending upon what perspective is used. There still remains, of course, the sharp definition of the city proper, but to which is now added the various layers of the metropolitan region it dominates, as well as the sometimes less-clearly visible extensions of those entities in the broader mix of interregional and even international activity. If shared political affiliations with the powers that be in Madrid are anything to go by, as they have been at times in Barcelona's recent past, then the prospect of better relations and more support may be in the offing. In March of 2004, propelled at least in part by public outcry against the occurrence and handling of the tragic terrorist bombing of a train in Madrid, in which 191 people perished just days before, the Socialists – under the youthful José Luis Rodríguez Zapatero – won the national election over the incumbent center-right PP, led by Aznar's successor – Mariano Rajoy.[38] From most accounts, this was a surprise and quickly changed Spain's political landscape and the tenor of its foreign alliances. How the new government deals with regionalism, of which Barcelona and Catalonia are still a part, remains to be seen. As one prominent foreign journal put it, "a large proportion of Spaniards, it seems, want to live in a plural state of several nationalities, whereas another large proportion see their country as a unitary state infested by tiresome regional romantics."[39] However, in the case of Barcelona the older Maragall is no stranger to the younger Zapatero, nor are others in the local and national branches of the party. Moreover, socialists in Barcelona, unless sorely pushed, seem to place far less stock in the issue of regional identity per se than they do in the broader project of society building and, in the case of Maragall, broader networking with Europe and beyond.

End of an Era

As far as these latest turn of events is concerned, including the regional dynamics taking place in and around Barcelona, an era in the subject of concerted city building over the past quarter century can be seen to have come to an end. Or, to put matters another way, a chapter has closed sufficiently in the Barcelona story to allow a different kind of entity – a metropolis – to require further narration. If nothing else, it is certainly where the most interest now lies and will continue to lie in the future. This partial closure, or transition, is also not so much a matter of the 'facts on the ground,' to use an earlier turn of phrase, because change in this new direction has been occurring for some time, as it is one of collective mindset and attribution. The sense of a unifying geography has become enlarged, both by way of expanding spatial boundaries and by way of other socio-cultural and economic attributes that are now included. Official attitudes, often slow to respond in such circumstances, are also nudging forward in this same direction. Commonplace answers to the question: "what and where is Barcelona?" are changing and becoming less circumscribed. When asked, for instance, where they are from, someone living outside the city but in the metropolis, is likely to respond that they are from Barcelona. Indeed, as a young Catalan colleague put it recently "being from Barcelona is now something you want to put on your *resumé*" – a matter of special status and importance. In the past this may also have been the case, for Barcelona has exerted a certain charismatic hold over the region, but the response more likely would have come with more qualifications – like 'nearby,' in the 'vicinity of,' or 'generally speaking' – and not be made so casually and matter of factly nor, perhaps, with quite the same pride. This change of immediate attribution is probably especially the case for newcomers, either through migration into or within the region, of which there have been many, and for those simply growing up in the place with less historical and experiential associations with a particular locale. Moreover, this transition and change does not portend the death of a city and the birth of a metropolis, as it sometimes has elsewhere. Rather, it is one in which the City of Barcelona's continued prosperity and success – as stated many times in this text – resides palpably with the idea of 'metropolis' rather than that of 'city,' *per se*, and, indeed, *vice versa*. This doesn't mean, however, that new building and spectacular projects in the city are a thing of the past, for this seems unlikely, given Barcelona's sustained and historical commitment to urban-architectural excellence and its continuing and even more central role in the region. Most of what's planned to be built will probably be built, and further rounds of renewal, renovation and 'filling in the gaps,' so to speak, seem likely to continue to occur, even in conjunction with more recent projects. Also, heightened definition of Barcelona's role in its region will, no doubt, spark new project ideas and initiatives. By contrast with the immediate past, however, what this change in perception does mean is that the city's urban projects and initiatives will take place in a broader framework and likely with different, probably less precious qualities of significance and import. If this occurs, Maragall and like-minded officials will also probably have their wish of not having to be the 'capital of something every fifteen years' and, with it, at least some major reasons for the sharp, episodic tempo of Barcelona's urban-development over recent years will dissipate and probably favor a more sustained trajectory.

Lately, Barcelona also appears to be moving into an era when more political attention needs to be focused on social issues like crime, immigration and education, as well as on environmental issues, all of which don't stop at the city's borders, as noted earlier, and will also require substantial degrees of inter-governmental co-operation. In addition, the need for physical rehabilitation of housing and other capital improvements appears to be more pressing, shifting the emphasis away from the glitz of brand new construction. Largely ignored for some time, housing provision per se has become an important social concern once again, as elsewhere in many parts of Europe. Sharply declining interest rates, sharp increases in employment opportunities and a relatively low turnover in housing have pushed up demand in the Barcelona metropolitan area, especially in or close to the city, as well as market prices for housing. For some knowledgeable observers, government-assisted housing is fast becoming the future issue for Barcelona to resolve. In practice, this seems likely to require a consistently high throughput of affordable supply concomitant with needed liberalization of mortgage lending practices away from individuals towards dwelling units as assets of collateral. As noted earlier, in the recent past Barcelona's housing production has been high – as much as 9 dwelling units per thousand population. However, it has also not been consistently high over an extended period, even with moderate to high pent-up demand, further suggesting the need for financial reform and more fluidity in the market place. In any event, plans are afoot to provide around 100,000 new housing units over the next ten or so years, with early locations in and around Sagrera, Besòs and towards the Zona Franca.[40] At present, considerable housing replacement has been occurring in the Ciutat Vella, to the north-east of Via Laietana, among other areas of the city. However, new sites will also need to be found and, given the volume of projected supply, most will be outside of the city proper and in the broader metropolitan area.

The shift in stance from city to metropolis is also yet another instance of expanding ambition and expanding vision, that follows in a well-trodden path. Breaking out of the walls, both literally and metaphorically occurred during the 1850s, followed later by annexation of outlying towns, and then by sheer peripheral expansion. Far more recently, to reiterate further, there was the shift in emphasis on localized, more-concentrated urban intervention, characteristic of the 1980s, to the more encompassing metropolitan vision that accompanied preparation for the Olympic Games and large-scale infrastructure development.

Today, now that the issue of Barcelona in its broader urban region and beyond is beginning to be addressed, the process and more expansive perception of Barcelona in its world continues. In most if not all instances, these and other expansions of ambition and vision have been common undertakings shared by those in government, civil society and the private sector. In fact, in many cases they were led by private interests or influences brought to bear on local officials, just as in other cases leadership came from public authorities. In all cases, however, they were joint-efforts, in one way or another, involving at least substantial elements of all three sectors. Furthermore, ambition and vision were not only directed towards furthering entrepreneurial and economic social well-being, but also towards unabashed cultural advancement and distinction, such as the 'city as a work of art,' or the 'city as a cultural capital,' if only for a moment, which almost everyone seemed willing to buy into. Moreover, these expansive ambitions and visions were also pushed on Barcelona by outside, political, social and economic events, and were not entirely of their own making. The various 'breakouts,' if they can be called that, were usually occasioned by prior periods when there was a strong cultural sense of competition and even repression from the outside. Further, often in these cases, a collective desire to be different, or somehow appear to be different, from others in Spain and particularly from those in Madrid, almost instinctively seems to have pushed and even continues to push, indigenous thinking about the place and role of Barcelona in a strongly outward direction.

Looking back over the city-building and the formative period of metropolitan expansion that took place, roughly from 1979 to 2004, much has been accomplished. Briefly, without trying to exhaustively repeat various statistics of success cited earlier, most of the city has been refurbished in one way or another, often extensively. Barcelona's 'cultural engine,' so to speak, has been overhauled, restarted and revved up. Many public service needs of the population have been met, even if some are re-appearing. People, for the most part, certainly enjoy higher standards of living and the general quality of amenities in the city have vastly improved. Barcelona is also more economically robust and competitive than it had been at other times in the past, and a more attractive venue for tourists, sojourners and outside investors. To be sure, more needs to be accomplished and, no doubt, will continue to be needed. Again, without repeating what has already been said in this regard, attention needs to be paid to: changing populations; environmental cleanup; adjustment of the balance of productive versus less-productive economic activities; employment opportunities;

and mobility, both physically and socially. Nevertheless, on par, Barcelona is generally regarded as a success story and, not undeservedly, widely regarded as one of the 'darlings,' as it were, of urbanists and observers of good government in various parts of the world.[41]

Also looking back over the city-building process of the past quarter century, the strong parallels with Barcelona's rebirth – *renaixença* – during the second half of the nineteenth century and early part of the twentieth century, alluded to in this book's introduction, are now more explicitly visible. Both periods were historically episodic in general character, made up of actions and reactions, as well as flurries of civic activity and slow downs. The strategy of inventing pretexts for grander visions and projects for the city repeated itself, most notably with the International Exhibitions of 1888 and 1929 and the Olympic Games of 1992, followed by the Cultural Forum and collateral activities of 2004. All were clearly aimed at international audiences and at burnishing Barcelona's image on the international stage. During both periods, Barcelona emerged from dire social and only somewhat less dire economic circumstances. Further cultural and intellectual rehearsal, followed by civic action, took place during critical moments between repression and self-determination. Also, internal tensions, if not outright struggles, existed or took place between conservatives and progressives, again during both periods. In addition and of importance to this text, architecture and urban expression were seized upon on both occasions, as part of the modern means forward and to manifest what had been achieved and to guide and give palpable shape to broader visions. Despite these similarities, however, history rarely, if ever, repeats itself. The recent re-incarnation of Barcelona, for instance, was not marked, except perhaps at the beginning, by such moments of civil violence and brutality as was the earlier period of re-birth. Absent, also, was much in the way of cultural nostalgia, backward-looking folk lore and national-regional essentialism that pre-occupied so many in the earlier period. On the contrary, if anything, an almost entirely contemporary, forward-leaning cultural outlook characterizes today's Barcelona. No doubt, differences in dominant political positions, like the *Lliga* as compared to the present socialists, also came into play on such matters of taste, representation, identity and presumed cultural heritage. Furthermore, the buffeting of Barcelona from external events was far less evident during the recent period, when compared with the former, in large part due to the less ambiguous socio-political trajectories of those around, even when viewed from specific moments during each of the two periods.

Catalanism variously defined, one of the bulwarks of the region during embattled times, if not as much in Barcelona, is neither as marked now, nor as rampant, nor as tied to conservative, rural and dogmatic church interests as it has been in prior eras. Nevertheless, common strains clearly persist. Catalan is the language of government and much of business. Many cultural and civic institutions conserve Catalan heritage and advance modes of expression with traditional roots, or presences, in contemporary cultural life. Mores and manners of daily life, not to mention cuisine, are also inflected, happily it would often seem, by belonging – in the mind's eye of those who deploy them – to Catalonia. So-called 'branding' and 'labeling' in the economic sector also now often trades heavily on associations with Barcelona and, although this is a far cry from 'Catalanism' as usually understood, indeed it could be contrary, such associations can also carry a strong regional flavor. Moreover, collective senses of independence and pride, certainly not uncharacteristic of Barcelonians and not in any belligerent, nor anti-Spanish, nor anti-internationalist manner, also often issue forth from a Catalan sense of self-identification. Possibly, as in other parts of the world where strong regional cultural sensibilities have existed, erosion will take place. However, in Barcelona it's not clear why such sensibilities shouldn't persist. If they don't impede, why not? If this cultural self identification, in addition to other forms of positive identity construction, adds personal value, why not? If nothing else, common local language, even more so than dialect, as well as other local cultural attributes that have also been entrained, including manners of city building, are powerful ways of constructively and humanely resisting the banal leveling effects of modernization without necessarily impeding progress. Indeed, this was profoundly indicated by Pasolini and other intellectuals early on, when the onslaught of the modern project finally hit southern Europe after World War II. In Barcelona and Spain, where there were further interruptions and delays, much the same point can and, no doubt, has been made. Then too, there is that commonly-praised other quality of self-identification – *seny* – that apparently goes with being Catalan, as mentioned earlier, variously defined as being commonsensical, hard-working, independent, sometimes sentimental, practical and perhaps a little shrewd. Much as generalizations of this kind are difficult if not impossible to really sustain and perhaps should not be indulged in at all by way of explanation, the presence of *seny*, nevertheless, can be seen in the combination of inspired and yet pragmatic approaches to reconstruction in Barcelona. When push came to shove, it was rather clearly manifest in the manner of dealing with higher authorities and the minimization of local risk. It was also present in the gradualism in the build-up, over time, of approaches to reconstruction and in the sheer level of effort involved. However, this cannot be the whole story.

End of an Era

Just as clearly the strides taken in Barcelona's redevelopment required levels of leadership and vision almost in spite of inherent characteristics of *seny*, in order to move beyond the other side of the trait, including being overly thrifty, lacking broad vision, constantly requiring tangible results, and ultimately being rather timid with regard to broader entrepreneurial opportunities. Moreover, this in itself, was an accomplishment and again shows how intrinsic cultural circumstances have matured, changed and become far less hegemonic than they were in the past.

Another conspicuous aspect of the recent and present period in Barcelona, is the continued presence of a socialist dominated municipal government. The PSC – *Partito Socialista de Catalunya* – has held sway there, through seven terms, from 1979 to the present day, with three mayors – Narcís Serra from 1979 to 1983, Pasqual Maragall from 1983 to 1999, and Joan Clos from 1999 to now. It is at least one of the longest, if not the longest, tenures of a socialist government in a large European city, and the major force behind the reconstruction and building of Barcelona. To be sure, this has actually been a coalition, always with the Communist Catalan Party and now with the ERC in the last two periods. In fact, this arrangement seems to have been more productive because of the negotiations required, rather than the PSC having it all their own way. Nevertheless, by political persuasion, the PSC is very much a party of the so-called 'New Left,' as noted earlier, even before the phrase took on popular traction. There is belief in the benefits of free trade, competitive economic markets and an openness towards and a sense of partnership with the private sector. At times the municipal government could be seen, for instance, in the unusual position of feeling it necessary to encourage private-sector entrepreneurial action. But, there is also a strong belief that government should take initiative, assume responsibility and lead the city, especially on issues involving social justice, public health safety and welfare, service provision, and, not coincidentally, in matters of urban reconstruction and city building. Barcelona's three mayors have all been concerned with, and directly engaged in, urban projects sponsored by the city and each one has had a feeling of personal responsibility for what Joan Clos, as noted earlier, called urban architecture as the 'handwriting of the city.' Maragall, in particular has a strong academic background in urban economics and planning and, although Clos is a medical doctor by professional background, his specialty is epidemiology and, therefore, he is especially knowledgeably concerned with populations and their public health and related living conditions. By and large, the socialists have enjoyed a not unexpectedly strong rapport with governmental, non-governmental and 'grass-roots' groups at district and neighborhood levels, especially among the working and lower-middle classes, although they have also earned wide respect among other more affluent segments of society. In fact, as narrated earlier, while shifting back and forth between the 'center left' and the 'center right' at the national level, the Barcelona electorate has remained relatively steadfast in their support of the socialists at the municipal level as the government most likely to run the city well, or at least not badly. There have, of course, been ups and downs in the socialists electoral popularity, usually and again not unexpectedly fluctuating with macro-economic circumstances, employment opportunities and the like, and recently allegedly because of what many perceived to be overly-ambitious public projects. But the party has remained in power.

Beyond these generalities, there are several distinctive features of Barcelona's socialist-led government that also warrant comment as keys to their success. First, there is a strong problem-solving orientation within the municipal authorities, and by large, they have been ably staffed at the bureaucratic level. Evidence of this orientation can be found, for instance, in the pattern of specific council posts, established during each regime and ranging in number and fineness of scope, depending on the content of perceived tasks at hand, from as little as 10 during Maragall's tenure between 1983 and 1987, to as many as 21 and more, in more recent times, as the complexity of oversight and managerial functions has increased. At an administrative level, the government has also been well served by interlocking responsibilities in search of higher degrees of co-ordination and efficiency, especially during times when capital and other projects needed to move forward. The combination of all infrastructure, urban and architectural considerations, for instance, under Josep Acebillo, during Mayor Clos' recent regime is a case in point. Second, the municipal government has always adopted a pro-active stance of looking out for and seeking outside opportunities for economic, social and cultural advancement of the city. Moreover, they have been rather good at it, judging from the Olympics, Fòrum 2004, the high-speed train installations, and expansion of other key facilities. In this regard, they often seem to act as a highly-entrepreneurial government corporation, without the negative connotations that often follow from corporate state enterprise. Third and as a corollary to this pro-active stance, the municipal government, often with the support, it must be said, of the Generalitat, has been relatively successful in making Barcelona's case to the national government in Madrid. When it's all said and done, particularly given the long history of tension between Madrid and Barcelona, this strong, yet judicious, lobbying effort has been remarkable in gaining vital resources and support, even if in other more relaxed circumstances it might have also been expected. Fourth and again much in the same regard, the socialist's view in Barcelona of the regional nationalist issue has been relatively mute, especially by comparison to the voice of the earlier conservative government in the Generalitat. Further, it might also be said, in relationship to the powers that be in Madrid, that it takes 'two to tango,' or, in this context, truly rumba. However, the intricacy of this dance cannot occur when one partner is well out of step with the other. Finally, the socialists in Barcelona have shown a remarkable ability to sound a popular rallying call at appropriate moments. As noted in chapter one and in chapter four, the city's leadership has been successful in inculcating a sense of collective urgency, opportunity and even crisis – replete with fiestas and political rumba parties – in order to take on new projects and under the guise that Barcelona will fall behind without these efforts. Clearly this has been an appeal to local pride and also trades on elements of Catalan self-identification and comparative distinctions between 'us and them.' Oddly although not consciously, it also takes something out of Singapore's political 'play book' where a so-called 'siege mentality' has been harnessed to strive and make real progress towards a tropical city of excellence. The potential force of this kind of appeal, however, may also be waining in Barcelona, through influxes of immigrants and corresponding declines in the numbers of inhabitants with close Catalan self-identification, as well as the broader and more diffuse contemporary concept – referred to earlier – of Barcelona as a place.

More specifically with regard to Barcelona's reconstruction and building, a *modus operandi* has been developed within the municipal government, also with specific and distinctive features. First, strong technical leadership has been a driving force, in combination with and in direct connection to strong political leadership at the mayoral level. From the beginning, a strong alliance was formed between the socialist government and broad segments of the academic and professional communities. As Maragall put it, "the best solutions result from this arrangement."[42] This alliance and the forward and critical thinking that goes with it, especially prompted from the academic and interrelated professional side, has also persistently placed the municipal government in a position to have potential solutions prepared ahead of popular perceptions of problems. It has also shaped the intellectual and technical background sufficiently around urban issues and needs and in a manner that has facilitated relatively immediate association with external opportunities and pretexts for city building. Second, instrumentally, at least since around 1987, Barcelona has relied on

SAs – *societats anònimes* – or limited public companies, to manage and see through public projects. Although there has been some grumbling about the transparency of these operations, as mentioned earlier, even though they are a matter of public record, they have proven to be efficient mechanisms for project delivery, by tailoring personnel to the scale and expertise required, as well as by observing finite time limits on their usefulness. These characteristics have also allowed the municipal government to avoid inflated and burgeoning technical bureaucracies and allowed reasonably constant recruitment of able younger talents into government service. Historically, as noted earlier, they also delve back into Barcelona's more distant past on the private sector side. Third, both as an enlargement and corollary to the presence of SAs, the formation of strong technical support within public entities like IMPUSA and, now, Barcelona Regional continues to provide a useful, non-politicized source of comprehensive information and a capacity to both sufficiently and effectively shape specific projects prior to their subsequent realization. Recent extension of this technical service to a broader range of municipal and public agency functions, beyond the structure of specific SAs, also seems likely to foster higher degrees of public co-ordination and authority, so long as those providing the service do not, as it were, 'overplay their hand.' Fourth, considerable clarity, together with negotiation and even experimentation, was brought to bear on public-private project engagements. Although there was no illusion about the strength of public leadership in the jointed nature of project ventures, private participation was usually offered early in conceptualization and testing of project feasibility. At least one example occurred during the formative stages of the current 22@BCN effort in Poblenou, as described in chapter four, when master planning and urban design guidelines were being formulated and test cases set up with interested prospective entrepreneurs to explore possible outcomes. Fifth, the municipality has consistently sought out and nurtured local, often younger, design talent. This was particularly so during earlier days and has slackened off recently as the city has stepped on something of a bandwagon of engaging well-known international talent. In retrospect, though, and with exceptions, local designers seem to have done the most for the city through their contributions, saying something about Barcelona's unique urban characteristics and its almost subliminal cultural cohesion. Sixth, the city has owned large numbers of tracts within the city and has had access to others. As described earlier, this was one of the bases for the urban improvements in the 1980s and persists today, offering a strong point of leverage. For some time now, the city has also adopted a position of high visibility and promotion for its urban projects, almost again along corporate lines, although also, no doubt, in the interests of public disclosure and rallying popular support. In short, the *modus operandi* towards city building has been rather more corporate than traditionally bureaucratic, relied on a strong alliance with broad segments of academic and related professional circles, and, while inviting private sector participation and support, has operated with its own strong and well-fleshed-out agenda.

Throughout this text, the often conflicted relationship of Barcelona *vis a vis* the powers that be in Madrid and, therefore, the national government of Spain, have been commented upon. Therefore, there is no need for detailed accounts at this juncture. Barcelona benefited from immigration from elsewhere in Spain, principally as needed labor for its industrial enterprises. More recently, it has similarly benefited from those with a higher degree of technical wherewithal. Also, in Spain, Barcelona had an empire to exploit for more local gain and now there is Spain's broad umbrella for enticing capital investment, even as the city becomes economically less nationally dependent. Spain benefited, although not often noticed, by Barcelona as a leading force in democratic reforms and republican government and by the city's efforts to shed progressive light during moments of modernization. Also, Spain had and still has an economic powerhouse in Barcelona, capable of bringing further wealth and prestige to the nation. In the end, it probably is in Spain's interests to allow Barcelona to develop more fully and in Barcelona's interests to have Spain partake in these efforts and share the risk. Nevertheless, Barcelona must also recognize that alleged unfair treatment is also part of a nation-building exercise and continue to seek common cause, while also pursuing a broader international agenda which, if appropriately pulled off, will be to everyone's benefit – the expanding vision that is already in play.

Finally, returning to some earlier points, especially those raised in the last chapter, many in Barcelona seem to have reached the end of their tether with regard to large urban projects and interventions. As noted, part of the reason for this is probably because they are relatively comfortable in the present scheme of things and don't understand, as quickly as they might have in the past, the alleged importance of such undertakings. Its also a matter of the coherence of a collective vision. The perceptible scale and tangible aspect of the city as a unique place has enabled those who live and operate within it to believe that they were in reach of perfectibility, through concerted design effort and conscientious city building. Moreover, through an often courageous and opportunistic step-wise process, that periodically upped the ante and widened the scope of an urban vision capable of being quickly shared with both enthusiasm and verve, Barcelona has managed to close in on this idea of perfectibility. Also, during the same process, the so-called 'Barcelona model' of urbanization gained widespread international attention, if not envy. Just how applicable it might be elsewhere is a matter of conjecture, especially when viewed from an inside perspective tied to place, time and circumstances, as well as to a singular and downright quirkiness of underlying and evolving culture. It may also not prove to be entirely sustainable in the broader Barcelona region either, at least in one technical respect. Over time, planning authorities in Barcelona have become very adept at working backward and forward between larger planning frameworks and specific projects. Further, part of this success has relied on a readily appreciable underlying logic and poetic of spatial development that was drawn variously from Cerdà, Puig i Cadafalch and, recently, from Bohigas. However, the scale, diversity and dispersion of the greater Barcelona region is a different set of physical circumstances, as described at some length. Further successful practice of the same strategy will undoubtedly depend upon how city building issues are parsed, or broken down, and what can be imagined for the spaces in between. More positively, the remarkable continuity of municipality governance, both at the electoral level and within various authorities, has benefited the city profoundly, although surely its roots also lie in the sheer quality and dedication of those in charge and the technical wherewithal that was mustered. Further, the future key to the broader region's success will likely continue to reside in the 'know-how,' experience and verve of the City of Barcelona. However, now that the opportunity and even necessity of yet another expansion of vision is beginning to either present or force itself on Barcelona – due in no small part to the city's own success – the present era and this account are drawing to a close. Nevertheless, one thing seems to be relatively certain, a little like the never-ending story, those in Barcelona will continue to try to break out of its 'walls' – real, virtual and imaginary – as they have in the past.

HIGH ABOVE THE CITY .... *'signs of prowess and faith'*

Poble Sec

Poble Sec

View to the North-East

Torre Colón

Torre Agbar

Communications Tower on the Collserola

Barri Gòtic

FROM HERE TO THERE .... *'by ships and planes, and cars and trains.'*

Cinturó Litoral at Besòs

El Nus de la Trinitat

Ronda de Dalt

Ronda de Dalt

Ronda del Litoral

Park at Poblenou, beside the Ronda del Litoral

Moll de la Fusta

Sagrera

Zona Franca and El Prat Airport

REFERENCES

EARLIER MOMENTS

1 As described, for instance, by what the poet Antonio Machado called 'the two Spains.'
2 Robert Hughes. 1993. *Barcelona* (New York: Vintage Books), p. 234.
3 Joan Busquets. 2004. *Barcelona: La construcción urbanística de una ciudad compacta* (Barcelona: Ediciones del Serbal), pp. 86-88.
4 Hughes, *Barcelona*, p. 285 and Antoni Nicolau and Albert Cubeles, eds. 2004. *Abajo Las Murallas* (Barcelona: Ajuntament de Barcelona), pp. 138-146.
5 Busquets, Barcelona, pp. 124-125, and Ferran Sagarra i Trias, 'Les idees per a l'Eixample,' in Nicolau and Cubeles, *Abajo Las Murallas*, p. 88.
6 Busquets, Op. Cit., pp. 68-71
7 Joan Busquets i Grau, Miquel Corominas i Ayala, Xabier Eizaguirre i Garaitogoitia and Joaquim Sabaté i Bel. 1992. *Readings on Cerdà and the Extension Plan of Barcelona* (Barcelona: MOPT, Ajuntament de Barcelona and Secretaría General Técnica), p. 129.
8 Hughes, *Barcelona*, pp. 260-262.
9 Op. Cit., p. 279.
10 Busquets, et.al., Readings on Cerdà, and Hughes, *Barcelona*, pp. 284-285.
11 Busquets, Op. Cit., p. 225.
12 Hughes, *Barcelona*, p. 283 and Jaume Fabre and Josep M. Huertas. 1989. *Barcelona: La construcció d'una ciutat* (Barcelona: Ajuntament de Barcelona), p. 21.
13 Albert Garcia Espuche. 1990. *El Quadrat d'Or: Centre de la Barcelona modernista* (Barcelona: Lunweg Editores), pp., 22, 36, 37 and 180.
14 Ignasi de Solà-Morales. 1992. *Fin de Siècle Architecture in Barcelona* (Barcelona: Editorial Gustavo Gili), p. 162f.
15 Hughes, *Barcelona*, pp. 254-257, and Ferran Sagarra. 1996. *Barcelona, Ciutat de Transició-1848-1868* (Barcelona: Institut d'Estudis Catalans).
16 Hughes, Op. Cit., p.375.
17 Ibid., pp. 236-237.
18 Ibid., pp. 228-235.
19 Ibid., p. 237.
20 Oriol Vergés and Josep Cruañas. 1991. *The Generalitat in the History of Catalonia* (Barcelona: Generalitat de Catalunya), pp. 54-56, and Hughes, *Barcelona*, pp. 239-244.
21 Hughes, Op. Cit., pp. 240-250.
22 Josep Lluís Mateo, ed. 1996. *Barcelona Contemporánea, 1856-1999* (Barcelona: Centre de Cultura Contemporània de Barcelona), pp. 45-46; Hughes, *Barcelona*, pp. 203-204 and Busquets, *Barcelona*, p. 122.
23 Hughes, *Barcelona*, pp. 218-221.
24 Op. Cit., p. 235, and A. Barey. 1980. *Barcelona: de la ciutat pre-industrial al fenòmen modernista* (Barcelona: La Gaya Ciència).
25 Ibid., pp. 326-328.
26 Vergés and Cruañas, *The Generalitat*, pp. 57-61.
27 Hughes, *Barcelona*, p. 506.
28 Vergés and Cruañas, *The Generalitat*, pp. 67-71.
29 Op. Cit., pp. 62-63 and Hughes *Barcelona*, p. 522.
30 Hughes, Op. Cit., pp. 522-523.
31 de Solà-Morales, *Fin de Siècle*, p. 13.
32 Busquets, *Barcelona*, pp. 193-196.
33 de Solà-Morales, *Fin de Siècle*, p. 130.
34 Manuel Gausa, Marta Cervelló and Maurici Pla. 2002. *Barcelona: A Guide to Its Modern Architecture, 1860-2002* (Barcelona: Actar and Ajuntament de Barcelona), p. D3.
35 Op. Cit.
36 Laura Vinca Masini. 1969. *Gaudí* (London: Hamlyn), p. 32.
37 Gausa, Cervelló and Pla, *Barcelona*, p. 33.
38 Manuel Guardia and Albert Garcia. 1992. *1888, 1929, Deux Expositions, une ambition* (Paris: Ed Autrement).
39 de Solà-Morales, *Fin de Siècle*, pp. 30-31.
40 Hughes, *Barcelona*, pp. 391-395.
41 de Solà-Morales, *Fin de Siècle*, p. 14.
42 Gausa, Cervelló and Pla, *Barcelona*, p. C3.
43 Pere Hereu. 1989. *Vers una arquitectura national* (Barcelona: UPC).
44 de Solà-Morales, *Fin de Siècle*, p. 16 and p. 39.
45 Op. Cit., p. 24.
46 Ibid, p. 19.
47 J.F. Ràfol. 1949. *Modernismo y modernistas* (Barcelona: Editoral Destuo).
48 Ibid, and Ignasi de Solà-Morales. 1980. *Eclecticismo y Vanguardia: El caso de la Arquitectura Moderna en Catalunya* (Barcelona: Gustavo Gili).
49 Lluís Domènech and Lourdes Figueres. 1989. *Lluís Domènech i Montaner i el director d'orquestra* (Barcelona: Fundació La Caixa). On the standing of the three architects, there is general agreement. See Hughes, *Barcelona*, p. 393 and 404, and Ignasi de Solà-Morales, *Fin de Siècle*.
50 Hughes, *Barcelona*, p. 398, and Gottfried Semper. 2004. *Style in the Technical and Tectonic Arts, or Practical Aesthetics* – Transl. (Los Angeles: Getty Research Institute).
51 Busquets, *Barcelona*, pp. 169-170.
52 Hughes, *Barcelona*, pp. 468-520 and George R. Collins. 1961. *Antoni Gaudí* (London: Butterworth).
53 de Solà-Morales, *Fin de Siècle*, p. 81 and pp. 85-86.
54 Masini, Gaudí.
55 de Solà-Morales, *Fin de Siècle*, p. 87.
56 Hughes, *Barcelona*, pp. 404-411.
57 de Solà-Morales, *Fin de Siècle*, p. 87.
58 Hughes, *Barcelona*, pp. 533-535 and Gausa, Cervelló and Pla, Barcelona, p. F3.
59 Isidre Molas. 1987. 'Barcelona, a European City,' in Michael Reaburn, ed. *Homage to Barcelona: The City and Its Arts, 1888-1929* (London: Arts Council of Great Britain), pp. 89-90.
60 Gausa, Cervelló and Pla, *Barcelona*, p. G3.
61 Busquets, *Barcelona*, pp. 221-230.
62 Vergés and Cruañas, *The Generalitat*, pp. 73-79.
63 Busquets, *Barcelona*, pp. 250-260, and Molas, 'Barcelona, a European City', p. 94.
64 John Hooper. 1987. *The Spaniards: A Portrait of the New Spain* (London: Penguin Books), p. 239.
65 Op. Cit., p. 22-24.
66 Ibid, p. 24.
67 Borja de Riquer and J.B. Culla. 1989. *El franquisme i la Transició Democràtica, 1939-1988.* (Barcelona: Edicions 62), p. 133.
68 http://www.gencat.es/historia/agen.htm
69 Mateo, *Barcelona Contemporánea*, p. 136.
70 Hooper, *The Spaniards*, p. 24.
71 Op. Cit., p. 26.

72 Busquets, *Barcelona*, pp. 269-270 and Amado Ferrer. 1996. 'The County Plan and the Codification of Urban Forms,' in Mateo, *Barcelona Contemporánea*, pp. 133-135.
73 Gausa, Cervelló and Pla, *Barcelona*, p. J3.
74 Macmillan Publishers. 2000. *The Grove Dictionary of Art* (London: Macmillan).
75 Hooper, *The Spaniards*, pp. 27-28.
76 Op. Cit., p. 28.
77 Ibid., p. 34.
78 Tomàs Vidal. 1996. 'Barcelonians: 1950,' in Mateo, *Barcelona Contemporánea*, pp. 115-118.
79 Hooper, *The Spaniards*, pp. 91-95.
80 Busquets, *Barcelona*, pp. 330-331.
81 Op. Cit., p. 334.
82 Hooper, *The Spaniards*, pp. 48-60.
83 Elecciones democráticas en España, http://web.jet.es/politica/21/eleccionesespana.htm.

COLLECTIVE POSSESSION

1 Joan Busquets. 2004. *Barcelona: La construcción urbanística de una ciudad compacta* (Barcelona: Ediciones del Serbal), pp. 329-331.
2 Joan Antoni Solans. 1996. 'General Metropolitan Plan of Barcelona,' in Josep Lluís Mateo, ed. *Barcelona Contemporánea, 1856-1999* (Barcelona: Centre de Cultura Contemporània de Barcelona), p. 205.
3 Op. Cit., pp. 203-205.
4 Ibid., p. 205.
5 Ibid., p. 205.
6 Manuel Gausa. 1996. 'Leap in Scale: From Urban to Metropolitan Barcelona,' in Mateo, *Barcelona Contemporánea*, p. 227. There is also perhaps some debate over the amount of property, with Solan's recalling a total of 56 hectares set aside inside the Municipality.
7 Ricard Pié. 1996. 'The General Metropolitan Plan of Barcelona,' in Mateo, *Barcelona Contemporánea*, pp. 207-209.
8 Op. Cit., p. 207.
9 Carlos Prieto. 1996. 'The Neighborhood Associations,' in Mateo, *Barcelona Contemporánea*, p. 189.
10 Manuel Naya. 1996. 'The Neighborhood Associations,' in Mateo, *Barcelona Contemporanea*, pp. 191-193.
11 Borja de Riquer and J.B. Culla. 1989. *El Franquisme i la Transició Democràtica, 1939-1988* (Barcelona: Edicions 62).
12 John Hooper. 1987. *The Spaniards: A Portrait of the New Spain* (London: Penguin), p. 179.
13 http://www.banrep.gov.co/augusta.htm, regarding Grupo de Barcelona.
14 For instance, Victor M. Pérez-Díaz. 1993. *The Return of Civil Society: The Emergence of Democratic Spain* (Cambridge, Massachusetts: Harvard University Press), p. 55.
15 Elecciones democraticas en España, http://web.jet.es/politica 21/eleccionespana.htm.
16 Hooper, *The Spaniards*, p. 40.
17 Electoral Data, http://www.bcn.es/estadistica/catala/cautev13/htm.
18 Serra Profile, http://www.congreso.es/diputados.
19 Biografías y Vidas, http://www/bigrafiasyvidas.com/bio.
20 Electoral Data, http://www.bcn.es/estadistica/catala/cautev13/htm.
21 Maragall, 9th International Design Award from http://www.jdf/award9a.ole.htm.
22 Félix de Azúa. 1982. 'Barcelona es el 'Titanic,' *El Pais*, viernes 14 de mayo de 1982, opinión, p. 13.
23 Interview with Eduardo Mendoza, the author of *La ciudad de los prodigos* among other works, on Wednesday, 18th December, 2002.
24 The following account of the urban public spaces of Barcelona is based on field observation and on: Joan Busquets. 1989. 'Scales of Activity,' *Rassegna*, 37, March, pp. 38-53; Peter G. Rowe. 1991. *The Urban Public Spaces of Barcelona, 1981-1987* (Cambridge, Massachusetts: Harvard University Graduate School of Design), and M. Cristina Tullio. 1987. *Spazi pubblici contemporanei: Innovazione e identita a Barcelona e in Catalogna* (Rome: Quaderini de Au, Editrice in ASA). Also, Peter G. Rowe. 1997. *Civic Realism* (Cambridge, Massachusetts: MIT Press), chapter 2.
25 Rowe, *The Urban Public Spaces of Barcelona*, p. 7f.
26 Ajuntament de Barcelona. 1987. *Barcelona: Spaces and Sculptures, 1982-1986* (Barcelona: Joan Miró Foundation).
27 Oriol Bohigas. 1986. *Reconstruction of Barcelona* (Madrid: MOPU Arquitectura). Also see Kenneth Frampton. 1985. *Martorell Bohigas and Mackay: 30 años de arquitectura, 1954-1984* (Madrid: Xarait Ediciones).
28 Peter Buchanan. 1989. 'Regenerating Barcelona with Parks and Plazas,' *Architectural Review*, June, pp. 32-46.
29 Manuel Vázquez Montalbán. 1992. *Barcelonas* (London: Verso).
30 Mendoza, Interview.

OLYMPIC OPPORTUNITY

1 *The Economist*. 1996. 'A Survey of Spain: In Transit,' The Economist, December 14, p. 5.
2 Olympic Games – Barcelona, http://www.kiat.net/olympics/history/25barcelona.html.
3 International Olympic Committee – Juan Antonio Samaranch, http://www.olympic.org/presidents/samaranch-uk.asp.
4 Manuel Gausa, Marta Cervelló and Maurici Pla. 2002. *Barcelona: A Guide to Its Modern Architecture, 1860-2002* (Barcelona: Actar and Ajuntament de Barcelona), p. 01.
5 Elecciones democraticas en España, http://web.jet.es/politica21/eleccionespana.htm.
6 Electoral data, http://www.bcn.es/estadistica/catala/cautev13.htm.
7 David Cohn. 1992. 'Pasqual Maragall, Mayor of Barcelona,' Architectural Record, August, pp. 112-113.
8 Lluís Serra. 1992. 'Management and Financing,' in Antoni Llagostera and Maria Lluïsa Selga, eds. *Olympic Barcelona the Renewed City* (Barcelona: Àmbit Servis Editorials, S.A.), pp. 35-39.
9 David Cohn. 1992. 'Building Barcelona,' *Architectural Record*, August, p. 100.
10 Op. Cit.
11 Llagostera and Selga, *Olympic Barcelona*.
12 Federico Correa. 1992. 'The Olympic Ring,' in Llagostera and Selga, *Olympic Barcelona*, pp. 117-126.
13 'Olympic Ring,' *Architectural Record*, August 1992, p. 102.
14 Op. Cit., p. 104.
15 Cohn, 'Building Barcelona,' p. 101.
16 Richard Ingersoll. 1992. 'Architectures of Olympic Barcelona: Journal of

a Post-Columbian Critic,' *Arquitectura y Vivienda*, 37, p. 102.
17   Op. Cit., p. 103.
18   Cohn, 'Building Barcelona,' p. 100.
19   Luis Fernández-Galiano. 1992. 'Viaje a Icaria,' *Arquitectura y Vivienda*, 37, p. 4.
20   Cohn, 'Building Barcelona,' p. 100.
21   Oriol Bohigas. 1992. 'A New Barcelona: Reflections on the Last Ten Years,' *Arquitectura y Vivienda*, 37, p. 98.
22   Ingersoll, 'Architectures of Olympic Barcelona,' p. 103.
23   Ignasi de Solà-Morales. 1992. 'Use and Abuse of the Historical City: Barcelona's Olympic Village,' *Arquitectura y Vivienda*, 37, p. 104.
24   Op. Cit., p. 105.
25   Ingersoll, 'Architectures of Olympic Barcelona,' p. 102.
26   de Solà-Morales, 'Use and Abuse,' p. 104.
27   As termed by Rem Koolhaas – Lecture, Graduate School of Design, Harvard University, November 2003.
28   A Survey of Spain, *The Economist*, p. 5.
29   Joan Trullén. 2000. *Local Government Report on the Barcelona Metropolitan Plan: Economic and Regional Postulates and Proposals* (Barcelona: Barcelona Regional), p. 27.
30   Electoral Data, p. 1.
31   Elecciones democráticas en España, p. 1.
32   Cohn, 'Building Barcelona,' p. 100.
33   David Cohn. 1996. 'Post-Games Private Development Keeps Faith With Olympic Spirit,' *Architectural Record*, July 6, p. 15.
34   Op. Cit., p. 15.
35   Tomàs Vidal. 1996. 'Barcelonians: From 1996 into the Future,' in Josep Lluís Mateo, ed., *Barcelona Contemporánea*, 1856-1999 (Barcelona: Centre de Cultura Contemporània de Barcelona), pp. 241-244.
36   Op. Cit.

BOLD TRANSFORMATIONS

1   Ajuntament de Barcelona. 2002. *Barcelona's Main Economic Indicators, Dynamics and International Position* – Briefing Package (Barcelona: Ajuntament de Barcelona), p. 1. See also Joan Trullén. 2002. *Local Government Report on the Barcelona Metropolitan Plan: Economic and Regional Postulates and Proposals* (Barcelona: Barcelona Regional), p. 15.
2   Elecciones democráticas en España, http://web.jet.es/politica21/eleccionespana.htm.
3   Electoral Data, http://www.bcn.es/estadistica/catal/canter13.htm.
4   Op. Cit, p. 2.
5   Interview with Mayor Joan Clos on the 25th of July, 2002.
6   Victorian Department of Infrastructure. 2002. Joan Clos i Matheu – Metropolis Profile, http://w.metropolit.org/.
7   Joan Clos, Interview.
8   Healey and Baker. 1998 and 2001. *European Cities Monitor: Europe's Top Cities* (London: Healey and Baker Marketing Department), pp. 5-7 and pp. 18-28.
9   Ajuntament de Barcelona, *Barcelona's Main Economic Indicators*, p. 17 and Joan Trullén. 2001. *La metròpoli de Barcelona cap a l'economia del coneixement: diagnosi econòmica i territorial de Barcelona 2001* (Barcelona: Ajuntament de Barcelona), p. 30.
10   Op. Cit., p. 1.
11   Ibid, p. 1.
12   *The Economist*. 1996. 'In Transit: A Survey of Spain,' *The Economist*, December 14th, p. 7.
13   Caixa Catalunya y del departamento de Economía Aplicada de la Universitat de Barcelona. 2004. 'Ranking por communidades,' *La Vanguardia*, 8th September, p. 67.
14   Ajuntament de Barcelona, Barcelona's Main Economic Indicators, p. 3.
15   For example, Manuel Castells. 2001. *The Internet Galaxy: Reflections on the Internet, Business and Society* (Oxford: Oxford University Press) and Saskia Sassen, ed. 2002. *Global Networks, Linked Cities* (New York: Routledge).
16   Interview with Josep Oliu i Creus, President of Banc Sabadell on the 25th of July, 2002.
17   Annalee Saxenian. 1996. *Regional Advantage: Culture and Competition in Silicon Valley and Route 128* (Cambridge, Massachusetts: Harvard University Press).
18   Op. Cit. and Martin Kenney and John Seely-Brown, eds. 2002. *Understanding Silicon Valley: The Anatomy of an Entrepreneurial Region* (Stanford: Stanford University Press).
19   E.M. Rogers and J.K. Larsen. 1984. Silicon Valley Fever (New York: Basic Books).
20   Op. Cit. and Paul Mackun. 2002. *Silicon Valley and Route 128: Two Faces of the American Technopolis*, http://www.netvalley.com/archives/mirrors/sr&128.html.
21   Ibid.
22   Saxenian, Regional Advantage, p. 29f.
23   S. Rosegrant and D. Laupe. 1992. Route 128 (New York: Basic Books).
24   Op. Cit., p. 52.
25   Mackun, *Silicon Valley and Route 128*, p. 4.
26   Bangalore, India – Your Complete Internet City Guide, http://www.bangalorenet.com/ and Sadan and Dhume. 2002. 'Hi-Tech Centers: Silicon Slugfest,' *Far Eastern Economic Review*, August, pp. 28-32.
27   About IIMB, http://wwwiimb.ernet.in/html.
28   The Economist Intelligence Unit, Ltd. 2002. *GE: Bringing Good Things to India*, http://db.eiu.com/.
29   The Economist Intelligence Unit, Ltd. 2002. Overblown, http://db.eiu.com/ and Frank B. Tipton. 2002. 'Bridging the Digital Divide in Southeast Asia,' *ASEAN Economic Bulletins*, April, pp. 1-14.
30   The Economist Intelligence Unit, Ltd. 2002. *China: Wrong Side of the Tracks*, http://db.eiu.com/.
31   Tipton, 'Bridging the Digital Divide,' p. 7.
32   Dennis Berman. 1997. 'New York's Silicon Alley: A Steep Road Ahead,' *Business Week*, August 25, pp. 4-5.
33   Mackun, *Silicon Valley and Route 128*, p. 4.
34   Manuel Villalante. 2004. 'Del creixement a la mobilitat sostenible,' in Ajuntament de Barcelona. 2004. *Barcelona 1979-2004, del desenvolupament a la ciutat de qualitat* (Barcelona: Ajuntament de Barcelona), pp. 45-61.
35   Op. Cit., p. 55.
36   Enric Tello. 2004. 'Barcelona 2004: Sostenible?,' in Ajuntament de Barcelona, Barcelona 1979-2004, pp. 230-233.
37   Ajuntament de Barcelona. 1999. Barcelona: New Projects (Barcelona: Ajuntament de Barcelona).
38   Joan Trullén. 1996. 'Barcelona, the Flexible City,' in Josep Lluís Mateo, ed. *Barcelona Contemporánea*, 1856-1996 (Barcelona: Centre de Cultura Contemporània de Barcelona), p. 251.

39 Ajuntament de Barcelona, Barcelona: New Projects, p. 23.
40 From data furnished in an exhibition of projects in Barcelona at the Edifici Fòrum, September 2004.
41 Interview with Josep Acebillo on 25th of July, 2002.
42 Op. Cit.
43 As quoted in 'El géiser que simboliza la nueva Barcelona,' *La Vanguardia* Cuadernos Cívicos, #05, 2004, p. 44.
44 Ajuntament de Barcelona, *Barcelona: New Projects*, p. 25.
45 Robert Hughes. 1992. *Barcelona* (New York: Vintage Books), p. 263.
46 Ajuntament de Barcelona, *Barcelona's Main Economic Indicators*, p. 7.
47 Ajuntament de Barcelona, *Barcelona: New Project*, p. 25.
48 Francesc Peirón. 2004. 'Una idea para culminar Barcelona,' *La Vanguardia* Cuadernos Cívicos, #05, pp. 32-36.
49 Lluís Permanyer. 2004. 'Grandiosidad interior,' *La Vanguardia*, 7 Septembre, p. 3, vivir.
50 'De Gran Via a gran bulevar,' *La Vanguardia* Cuadernos Cívicos, #05, 2004, p. 40.
51 Juli Esteban i Noguera. 2004. 'Els sistemes de comunicació i transport,' in Ajuntament de Barcelona, *Barcelona 1979-2004*, p. 60.
52 Joan Busquets, et al. 2003. *La Ciutat vella de Barcelona: un passat amb futur* (Barcelona: Ajuntament de Barcelona).
53 The Economist. 2004. 'The Second Transition: A Survey of Spain,' *The Economist*, June 26th, p. 10.
54 'La Unesco quiere que los próximos Fòrums respeten el espíritu de Barcelona,' *La Vanguardia*, 7th September, 2004, p. 3, vivir.
55 Ferrán Boiza. 2003. 'Los Peces chicos comen terreno a los grandes,' *El Mundo*, 25 May, http://www.elmundo.es/2003/espana/municipales/barcelona.html.

EXPANDING VISION

1 Data on boundary conditions, population areas and densities were drawn from an interview and briefing with Joan Trullén i Thomàs and Maria Morés from the Universitat Autònoma de Barcelona and the Ajuntament de Barcelona on July 26th, 2002. See also, Joan Trullén. 2001. *La metròpoli de Barcelona cap a l'economia del coneixement: diagnosi econòmica i territorial de Barcelona 2001* (Barcelona: Ajuntament de Barcelona), pp. 7-17 and Generalitat de Catalunya. 1995. *Atles de L'Euroregió: Catalunya, Languedoc-Roussillon, Midi-Pyrénées* (Barcelona: Generalitat de Catalunya).
2 Joan Trullén. 2002. *Estratègia econòmica i territori* (Barcelona: Dep. d'Economia Aplicada UAB), table titled 'El pes econòmic de Catalunya.'
3 Data from Caixa Catalunya and the Departmento de Economica Aplicada de la Universitat de Barcelona, as reported in *La Vanguardia*, 8 Septembre, 2004, p. 67.
4 Trullén, Estrategia econòmica, table titled 'El pes conomia de Catalunya: una visió europea.'
5 Op. Cit., table titled 'Fluxos de capital.'
6 Ibid., table titled 'Població ocupada per sectors: 2001.'
7 Gabinet Tècnic de Programació. 2005. *Distribució per usos del sostre construït a Madrid i Barcelona* (Barcelona: Ajuntament de Barcelona – internal memorandum).
8 Ibid., table titled 'Comerç exterior,' and Ajuntament de Barcelona. 2005. Distribució per usos del sostre construït a Madrid i Barcelona (Barcelona: Gabinet Tècnic de Programació), p. 4.
9 Joan Trullén. 2000. *Local Government Report on the Barcelona Metropolitan Plan: Economic and Regional Postulates and Proposals* (Barcelona: Barcelona Regional), pp. 25-26.
10 Op. Cit., table 5. 'Average Size of Businesses in Various World Cities.'
11 Giacomo Beccattini. 2000. *Prato: una storia esemplare dell'Italia dei distretti* (Bologna: Le Monier) and Bennett Harrison. 1994. *Lean and Mean: The Changing Landscape of Corporate Power in the Age of Flexibility* (New York: Basic Books).
12 Albert García Espuche. 1998. *Un siglo decisivo: Barcelona y Catalunya 1550-1640* (Barcelona: Alianza Editorial).
13 Trullén, Local Government Report, p. 28.
14 Trullén, Estratègia econòmica, table titled 'Metropolitanització de Catalunya.'
15 Trullén, Local Government Report, pp. 29-30.
16 The Economist. 2004. 'A Survey of Spain: The Second Transition,' *The Economist*, July 26th, p. 10.
17 Peter G. Rowe. 2005. *East Asian Modern: Shaping the Contemporary City* (London: Reaktion Press), pp. 50-55.
18 Trullén, Local Government Report, pp. 29-30.
19 Op. Cit., p. 28.
20 Richard T.T. Forman. 2004. *Mosaico territorial para la region metropolitana de Barcelona* (Barcelona: Editorial Gustavo Gili, S.A.).
21 Joan Trullén. 1996. 'Barcelona, the Flexible City' in Josep Lluís Mateo. ed. *Barcelona Contemporánea, 1856-1996* (Barcelona: Centre de Cultura Contemporània de Barcelona), p. 251.
22 Interview with staff at Barcelona Regional, 27 July 2002.
23 Op. Cit.
24 Trullén, Local Government Report, p. 15f.
25 Op. Cit., p. 18.
26 Ibid., p. 9.
27 Trullén, 'Barcelona, The Flexible City,' pp. 247-253.
28 Generalitat de Catalunya, *Atles de L'Euroregió*.
29 Trullén, Local Government Report, p. 8.
30 Ajuntament de Barcelona. 2002. *Barcelona's Main Economic Indicators, Dynamics and International Position* – Briefing Package (Barcelona: Ajuntament de Barcelona), p. 3, chart titled, 'Public Sector Investment.'
31 *The Economist*, 'The Second Transition,' p. 6.
32 Interview with Pasqual Maragall on 25 July 2002.
33 Op. Cit.
34 Trullén, Local Government Report.
35 Interview with Josep Acebillo on 1 April 2005.
36 Forman, *Mosaico territorial*.
37 http://en.wikipedia.org/wiki/Catalunya.
38 *The Economist*, 'The Second Transition,' p. 6.
39 Op. Cit., p. 5.
40 Interview with Joan Clos and Josep Acebillo on 1 April 2005.
41 *The Economist*, 'Special Supplement on the Future of Cities,' *The Economist*, 21 July 1995.
42 Interview with Pasqual Maragall on 25 July 2002.

NECESSARY ABSTRACTIONS

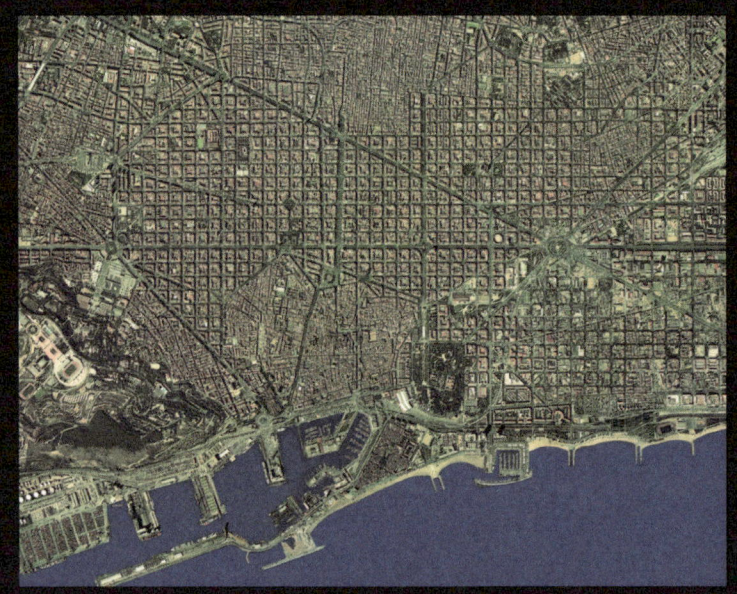

Cerdà's Eixample

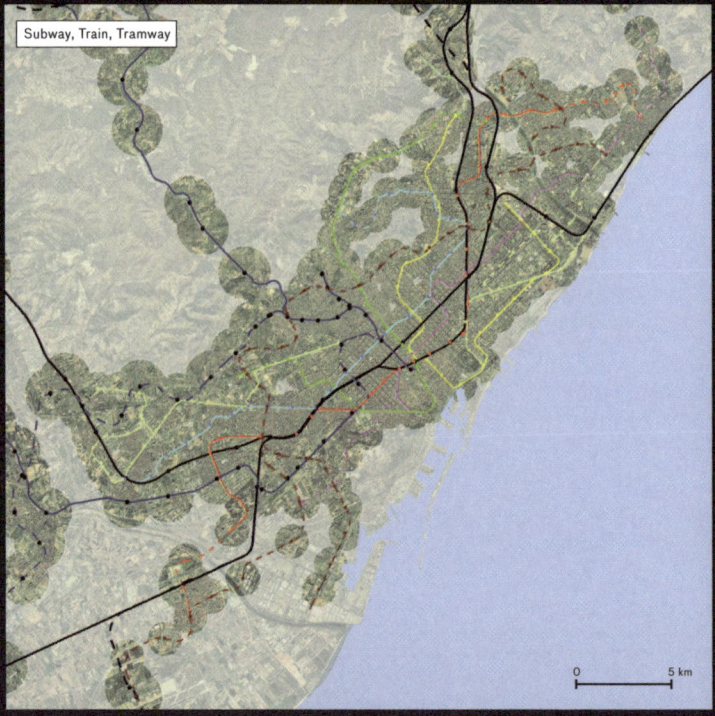

Subway, Train, Tramway

Transit Distribution

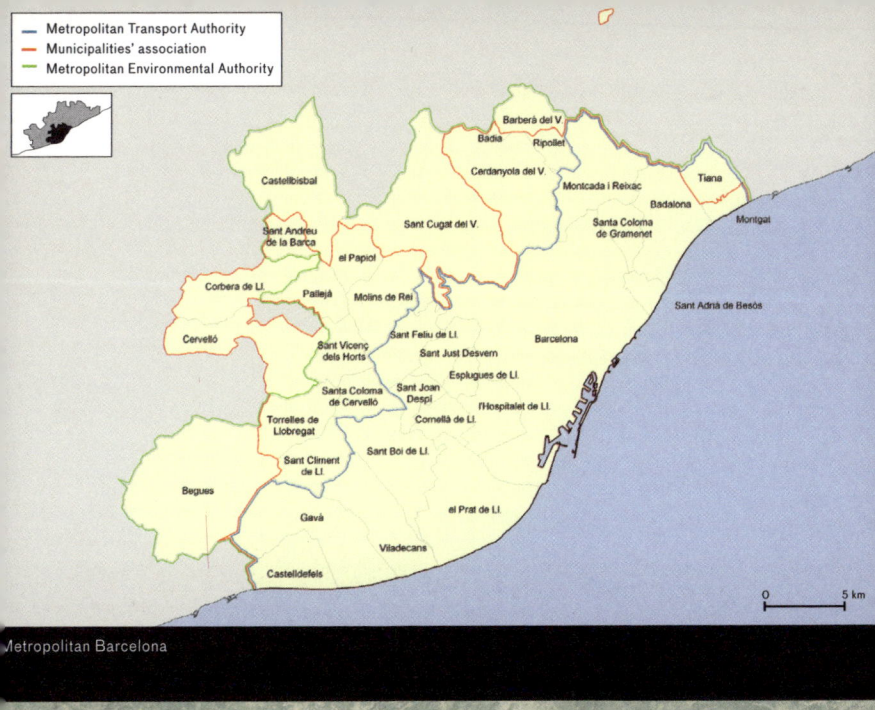

- Metropolitan Transport Authority
- Municipalities' association
- Metropolitan Environmental Authority

Castellbisbal
Sant Andreu de la Barca
Corbera de Ll.
Cervelló
el Papiol
Pallejà
Molins de Rei
Sant Vicenç dels Horts
Sant Feliu de Ll.
Santa Coloma de Cervelló
Sant Joan Despí
Torrelles de Llobregat
Sant Climent de Ll.
Sant Boi de Ll.
Begues
Gavà
Viladecans
Castelldefels
el Prat de Ll.
Cornellà de Ll.
l'Hospitalet de Ll.
Esplugues de Ll.
Sant Just Desvern
Barcelona
Sant Cugat del V.
Cerdanyola del V.
Badia
Ripollet
Barberà del V.
Montcada i Reixac
Santa Coloma de Gramenet
Badalona
Tiana
Montgat
Sant Adrià de Besòs

0   5 km

Metropolitan Barcelona

0   5 km

Metropolitan Region of Barcelona

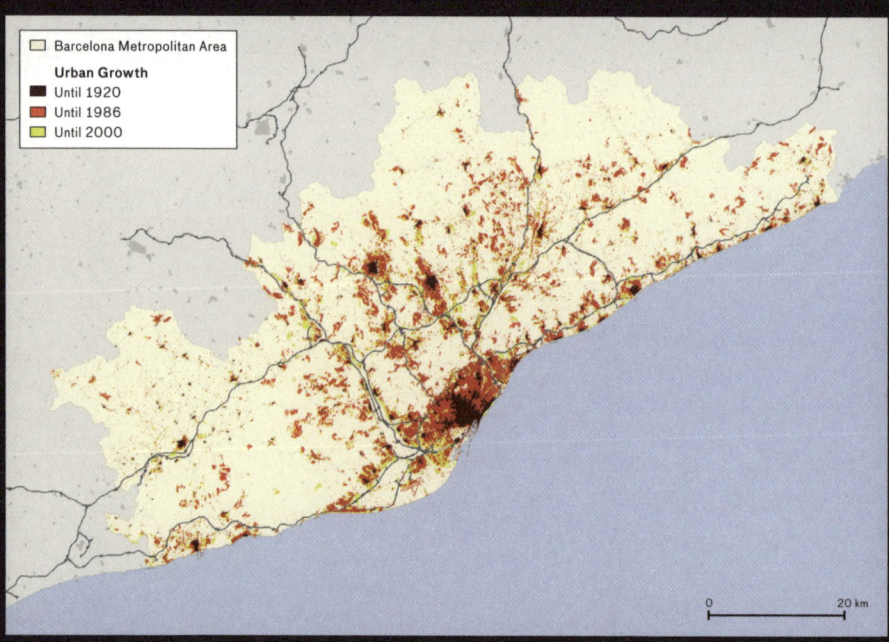

Urban Spread in the Metropolitan Region

- The emerald network
- Major food areas

Regional Environmental Landscape
from T. T. Forman's proposal: land Mosaic for the Great Barcelona Region, 2004

ILLUSTRATION CREDITS

Rosalía Vila and Dorote Boisot
Cover photograph and pages 39, 40, 41, 42 (bottom), 43, 46, 47, 74, 75, 76, 77, 78, 79 (top), 80, 81, 110 (bottom), 111, 112, 113, 114 (bottom), 115, 116, 117, 118, 119, 148, 149, 150, 151, 152, 154, 155, 156, 157, 188, 189, 190, 191, 192, 193, 194, 197, 198.

Wolfgang Weber
pages 71, 72, 114 (top)

Arxiu fotogràfic de l'Arxiu de la Ciutat de Barcelona
pages 38, 42 (top), 70, 73, 110 (top).

Jordi Todó, Tavisa
153 (bottom), 195, 196.

Barcelona Regional
pages 153 (top), 199, 204 (bottom), 205, 206, 207.

Oriol Rigat
pages 79 (bottom), 152 (top).

La Vanguardia Archive
pages 44, 45 (bottom)

Institut Cargogràfic de Catalunya
page 204 (top)

Published by
BARCELONA REGIONAL
ACTAR

Coordination
Eva Serra de la Figuera
Maria Buhigas

Graphic Design
Reinhard Steger

Digital Production
Carmen Galán
Oriol Rigat

Printing
Ingoprint S.A.

Distribution
ACTAR D
Roca i Batlle 2. E-08023 Barcelona
Tel +34 93 417 4993 Fax +34 93 418 6707
office@actar-d.com www.actar-d.com

© of the edition, BARCELONA REGIONAL and ACTAR, Barcelona 2006

BARCELONA REGIONAL
AGÈNCIA METROPOLITANA DE DESENVOLUPAMENT URBANÍSTIC I D'INFRASTRUCTURES S.A.
Tel +34 93 223 7400 Fax +34 93 223 7414
br@bcn-regional.com www.bcn-regional.com

ACTAR
Tel +34 93 418 7759 Fax +34 93 418 6707
info@actar-mail.com www.actar.es

© of the text, Peter G. Rowe
© of the images, their authors

All rights reserved

ISBN 84-96540-28-6
DL B-11887-06

Printed and bound in the European Union